FROM BROOMSTICKS
TO BATTLEFIEDS

FROM BROOMSTICKS TO BATTLEFIEDS

After the Battle:
The Story of Henry Clay Robinett

Bill Speer

WWW.DEEDSPUBLISHING.COM

Dedication

This book is dedicated to all the cadets of Delaware Military Academy, Pennsylvania Military Academy, and Pennsylvania Military College. Though the Corps may have passed into history it will always be in our hearts.

We are all still Colonel Hyatt's Riders!

Bill Speer
Class of '72

Table of Contents

The summer of 1968 was a year of transition for both our country and me. Newly graduated from Great Valley High School, I traveled with my parents to Chester, Pennsylvania, and I began my time as a "Rook" at Pennsylvania Military College. As I stepped through the looking glass, I had no idea just how much the next four years would change my life.

A Rook is the lowest rank of human (if indeed they are human) on earth. Those of you who were a Knob, Plebe, Rat, or Fish at a service academy or military college are nodding your heads in agreement at this point. Your days are not your own; they belong to the upper class cadre that are responsible for your training. As you brace in the corridors, do untold pushups, "step out" at 2230 hours, and complete countless other tasks designed to "break you down and then build you up," you slowly transform from a civilian into a cadet.

As my Rook handbook says, "The purpose of the Fourth Class Program is: ....To Familiarize Fourth Classmen with the history of Pennsylvania Military College, and with customs, ideals, and traditions of the Corps of Cadets." That is where this story begins. We were told of Henry Clay Robinett, Civil War hero, and graduate of our forefather, Delaware Military Academy. We were told of his great heroism at Corinth and of his eventual service on General Grant's staff. Indeed, we even had recently instituted "Battery Robinett," our artillery battery a few years before. I am sure there is not a PMC cadet alive today that does not recall the name.

My class (1972) was the last class of the Corps of Cadets. The Vietnam War and the Northern "climate" did us in, yet Robinett, as with most of our Rook training, stayed with me over the years as much as "How's the Cow" and other parts of our regimen. When the opportunity arose to visit the college (now Widener University) in 2008, I met with Rebecca Warda, collections manager of the PMC Museum and explored the possibility of a research project about Robinett, the school at the time, and what role its cadets played in the American Civil War. She was more than accommodating (and has since become a kindred spirit in this project) as we spent the day looking through the archives. Another day, she met me at the Delaware County Historical Society for some more exploratory work. Afterwards, I spent a few days at the Chester County Historical Society and the Delaware State Historical Society. I left Pennsylvania firmly convinced there was sufficient primary source material to begin the project.

At first, I was interested in working on Robinett and James Rush Lincoln, a classmate and friend of Henry's and a soldier in the Rebel Cause. Very quickly, it became obvious there was more to Robinett than met the eye, and I began to focus entirely upon him. As an adjunct at American Military University, I was pleased to learn they would assist me with a research grant (that I greatly appreciate), so I began in earnest.

Primary source materials drive research on historical events and figures, and I was lucky to find, with assistance, a wealth of information on Robinett and his experiences before, during, and after the war. At Widener University, the outstanding support and assistance provided by Rebecca Warda, PMC collections manager; Jan Alexander, Reference Librarian and University Archivist; and newly minted 2nd LT Keith Bright, Widener class of 2009 made this effort a success. When Becky's phone rings around 0900 she knows it is likely me. Jan helped me gain access to the Widener Archives without which this project would lack any understanding of the institutional history. Keith, a history major and member of the ROTC detachment, became my surrogate, making trips to numerous places for me. He found some wonderful information about Henry's church. I am deeply indebted to William Robinette, board member of the Robinett Family Association and database manager, for all his assistance throughout this project. His knowledge of Robinett lineage is incredible, and he has helped me flesh out the family picture. Worshipful Master Robert Benson, of the Lafayette Freemason Lodge, helped me place Henry in Freemasonry and explain his rapid progression therein. Trish Pritchard, University of the Pacific Library, Special Collections department, was a great help in getting Henry's letters organized. We spent many hours on the phone trying to read his handwriting, especially considering he wrote some letters horizontally, vertically, and diagonally! Special thanks to Raymond Nichols, volunteer at the Holy Trinity Church archives and Rebecca L. Wilson, Executive Director of the Old Swedes Foundation.   Keith, Becky, and I tramped around the cemetery looking for the grave of Henry's fiancé, and Rebecca gave us a wonderful tour of the church. The folks at the Delaware State Historical Society, especially Constance J. Cooper, Director of the Library at DHS, helped greatly in the past two years. I am also deeply beholden to Vonnie Zullos of Horse Soldiers Research. Since I am a fulltime military historian, under contract to the U.S. Army, her numerous trips to the National Archives on my behalf made this project possible; it would not exist, in its current form, without her.

Too many take for granted the astonishing people we have working for our National Parks. Tom Parson, Park Ranger at The Corinth Civil War Interpretive Center, spent a busy Saturday walking me around the field and helping me find materials in the archives. He also assisted in proofing the Corinth segment to make sure I was on the right track. Stacy D. Allen is Chief Ranger of Shiloh National Military Park and an expert on all matters Shiloh and Corinth and helped me understand the finer points of the engagement. I also appreciate the assistance of Terrence Winschel, Historian at Vicksburg National Military Park, in locating information on Robinett at Vicksburg. I would also like to thank Colonel Tommy Ryan, Louisiana National Guard Historian, for his assistance and the personal tour of Jackson Barracks in New Orleans. Ms. Allison Peña, Anthropologist for Jean Lafitte National Historical Park and Preserve helped me locate Robinett's gravesite and burial records. Dr. Bruce A. Leeson, Captain Kyle Grohmann, Dr. John Albrecht, and Ms. Susanne Jones at the Eisenhower Medical Center, Fort Gordon, Georgia, were of infinite assistance in understanding Robinett's state of mind. They all took time out of their busy schedules to spend hours with me, providing a "long distance" psychoanalysis of Henry.

I am also indebted to one of my graduate school professors, Joe Glatthaar. I was in Joe's very first graduate class at the University of Houston, and we have remained in touch since. His guidance and encouragement buoy my spirits every time I see him at the annual Society for Military History conference. Another military historian, Susannah Ural, whom I met at an American Historical Association conference as we dodged raindrops together, spent a good bit of time on the phone with me deciding if this project indeed held merit. Benjamin Franklin Cooling, a professor of mine at PMC, now at the Industrial College of the Armed Forces, inspired me back in 1968 with his encouragement and teaching style. One final academic needs special mention. Al Nofi and I have been friends for a long time. I knew him from his wargame design days and at one point, he accompanied my Junior Historians to Brackettville, TX and the "John Wayne" Alamo site. There, he took my students around the compound telling them wondrous vignettes and the story of the Alamo. Al also read a draft of this effort and provided numerous suggestions. Al tells me I owe him a beer since he wrote the Foreword for this piece; if we can ever manage to get in the same state, at the same time, drinks are on me!

Special thanks to Mr. and Mrs. Norman Taylor. Jeanne Taylor's aunt, Doris Robinette Favinger passed at the age of 92. As executors of the estate, they went through her house and found on the floor IN THE ATTIC, miraculously well-preserved papers belonging to Henry C. Robinett as well as his ceremonial saber. The papers included all of Robinett's commissioning documents, post cards with engravings of the battle of Corinth, genealogy pages from a family Bible, and a photo of Henry. They donated their discovery to the Delaware Historical Society just in time for Becky, Keith, and I to examine them. I must admit one of the greatest joys in conducting this venture was to actually hold Henry Robinett's saber in my hand and I am sure Keith feels the same.

Last but certainly not least, I would like to express my sincere gratitude to Sergeant Major (ret.) Jim Timmerman for all of his support and encouragement. Over the last four years, he has taught me more about the United States Army Signal Corps than anyone else as we worked together documenting the Global War on Terror. He read parts of this work and continues to be a very dear friend to this day.

A quick note on the format of this book. I chose to place detailed endnotes following each chapter. When I read, I like them there, so there you go! The writing is mine as are the mistakes, omissions, and inaccuracies. This is my first attempt at a serious publication, and I hope you will find it holds merit.

Foreword: Henry Clay Robinett

In the nearly microscopic print of Francis R. Heitman's *Historical Register and Dictionary of the United State Army* (Washington: 1903), the summary of Henry Clay Robinett's military career runs to little more than an inch:

> *Robinett, Henry Clay. Va. Del. 2 lt 1 inf 5 Aug 1861; 1 lt 23 Nov 1861; capt a d c vols 25 Mar 1864; hon dischd from vol ser 8 May 1865; dismd from U S A 29 Dec 1865; reinstd in 1 inf 24 Apr 1866; capt. 28 July 1866; bvt capt 4 Oct 1862 for gal and mer ser at the battle of Corinth Miss and maj 4 July 1863 for gal and mer ser dur the siege of Vicksburg Miss and bvt maj vols 9 Apr 1865 former ser in the campaign against the rebel army of northern Va commencing in front of Petersburg 29 Mar and ending 9 Apr 1865; died 22 Apr 1868*

While honorable, and, given his two brevets, even somewhat distinguished, Robinett's service seems little different from that of any other young man, North or South, who went off to war in 1861. At a glance, Robinett, who emerged from the war as a captain, would hardly seem a likely subject for a biography. Yet here we have just that, *From Broomsticks to Battlefields*, by my old friend Bill Speer.

In *From Broomsticks to Battlefields*, Bill has done something interesting. He has used Robinett's life to throw some light upon several aspects of the American experience and society in the mid-nineteenth century that have not yet been fully explored.

To begin with, of course, there's the biography of one of those many young men who went off to war, served honorably and well, with occasional moments of notable glory — in this case the defense of "Battery Robinett" during the Battle of Corinth (October 3-4, 1862) — and then, for those who survived, mostly went home and resumed their lives.

In Robinett's case, that meant a career in the Regular Army. That career, however, was marred by increasingly erratic behavior that ended in his suicide just three years after the war - the result of complex psychological problems that are carefully discussed in the book. *From Broomsticks to Battlefields* gives us a little more insight into the extent to which the horrors of war affect the personality and reminds us that historians and psychologists have barely begun to study the question of post-traumatic stress disorder among Civil War veterans.

From Broomsticks to Battlefields also opens a window on some of the social complexities of mid-nineteenth century America. Bill highlights what many historians, sociologists, and cultural anthropologists neglect: the importance of what the British used to call "interest" - the powerful effect that social, familial, and even religious ties could have on a person's pursuit of a successful career in business, politics, or even military service.

Finally, while much has been written about military education as a characteristic of Southern society, very little has been said about the subject of military training in the North. *From Broomsticks to Battlefields* reminds us that military education was not unknown in the North, as evidenced not only by such military institutions as Norwich Academy, the Peekskill Military Academy, or Delaware Military Academy, which became Pennsylvania Military Academy, Robinett's alma mater, but also by many academic institutions that had cadet companies, such as Bowdoin (Franklin Pierce once captained the corps of cadets, in which his friend Nathaniel Hawthorne served), Notre Dame, and others, as well as some military secondary schools, and several maritime academies, public and private, in the New England and Middle Atlantic states, that functioned along military lines

While giving us a look at the life of Henry Clay Robinett, Bill has also used that life to explore some important questions about American society in the mid-nineteenth century, no mean feat.

—Albert A. Nofi

Chapter I
"I believe I have been perfect and conducted myself properly"

"In order to fully comprehend the consequences of your decision in such a case, particularly if it be unfavorable to the accused, you must know the appropriate value and price of a Soldier's honor! A Soldier is the only man of all men, who feels himself rich indeed, 'when all but life and honor's lost!' But to the Soldier All things Else sink into insignificance in comparison to his honor!" [1]

By the time Henry Clay Robinett wrote these words he had aged well beyond his twenty-six years. Moving from boy to man in less than a decade, he experienced more challenges and obstacles than most do in a lifetime. His life reads like a classical Greek tragedy, with numerous antagonists ranging from a Confederate Colonel from Texas, fellow Union officers, and the United States Army, to even Henry himself. Robinett was not a model of perfection - neither a hero nor a villain. He was fundamentally a decent, good man who underwent significant changes and misfortune due to his experiences as a soldier in the Union army. Everything seemed to be moving his way in life when suddenly, after the war, his life-course reversed leading to a catastrophe of three courts martial and his eventual suicide. Henry C. Robinett was a victim of his overriding ambition, his sense of honor, character flaws, and physical conditions resulting from a serious war wound, as well as a post-war Army struggling to find its identity and mission.

1

Family Lineage

Born on June 20, 1841 into a decidedly middle class family his roots extend back to Allen Robinett, who emigrated from England to America in 1682 at fifty years of age. Allen was the first of his surname to settle in Pennsylvania and is the ancestor of nearly all who today bear variants of his name (Robinett, Robinette, Robnett) in the United States and Canada.[2]   Robinett's family could boast a long and proud military tradition as well. Henry's great-grandfather fought in a Virginia Regiment of the Line during the American Revolution. Allin Robinett, a great-grand uncle, also served in the Revolution in the first Continental regiment raised in Delaware. Joseph Robinett Sr., like his older brother Allin, served in various units during the Revolution. Robinett's grandfather, David Jr., is on the muster rolls of the Upper and Lower Chichester Townships militia in Pennsylvania during 1786/7. David Jr. became a shipmaster in the late 1790s, and commanded the revenue cutter *General Greene* in the early 1800s. Henry's granduncle, Jesse, served in Colonel Wall's Regiment of General Cocke's Brigade, Virginia Troops, in the War of 1812. Two cousins, once removed, also served in that war. Allen W. Robinett was in Blake's 2nd Mounted Volunteers during the Indian Wars in 1837 and 1838 while James T. joined the Confederate cause as a First Lieutenant with Perkins' Company (Fleet's Rifle Guard), Coston's Regiment (16th Virginia Volunteers), eventually serving in the Confederate Navy on board the *CSS Albemarle*. This rich and deep military heritage played a major role in Robinett's life. His ambition and desire to serve and his sense of duty, honor, and country, rooted within the branches of his family tree, moved him to attend Delaware Military Academy, where he rose to the rank of cadet Sergeant Major, and eventually to join the Union cause in the Civil War.[3]

Henry's father, Allen McLane Robinett, a clerk, along with his wife Susan and eight children moved about considerably in the years before 1850. From Virginia, where Henry C. was born, they went to Pennsylvania, and finally settled in Wilmington, Delaware. By 1860, the family was sufficiently positioned to sponsor an indentured servant, Margaret Wilson, who was an immigrant from Ireland.[4]   Brother, Allen, also served in the Civil War for various units, finally settling in as a sergeant in the 4th U.S. Infantry.[5] We know little about Henry's life until he began attending Delaware Military Academy at the age of fifteen in 1856 but can assume it was typical of the period; full of rambunctious, rough play and traditional schooling. Growing up in a border state gave him a unique view of the world and with the coming war, a sense of duty to his country instilled in him from family stories and DMA.

Delaware Military Academy

There is much written about a few notable military institutions such as VMI, The Citadel, Norwich, and of course, West Point, but little work has been done on antebellum, border state military institutions and their impact upon the war. Military education in the United States can point significantly to a single man for much of its inspiration and growth. Alden Partridge, an early superintendent of West Point, helped to establish numerous institutions including The American Literary, Scientific, and Military Academy (Norwich). It was his belief, that private military institutions became paramount to the safety of our nation by developing hundreds of young men who could organize and lead volunteer militias in times of emergency while at the same time providing these men with a classical and scientific education.[6]

John Bullock opened a boarding school for boys in Wilmington in 1821, and upon his death in 1847, Samuel Alsop ran the school until 1853 when Colonel Theodore Hyatt took over the school and dubbed it Hyatt's Select School for Boys. The military department began in 1858, and the school was renamed Delaware Military Academy in 1859. Two previous attempts to establish a military school in the state of Delaware failed after a year or two of trial.[7]

Theodore Hyatt was in charge of the Parochial School of the First Presbyterian Church of Wilmington when he purchased the equipment and "good will" of the Bullock school from Samuel

Alsop in 1853.   Born in Yorktown, New York in 1826, he spent his early years working on the farm. Buxton recounts an incident in his life that changed Hyatt forever:

The Presbyterian congregation at the place of his birth, were erecting a new church edifice, and a number of boys, including young Theodore, were in the habit of jumping on the stone drags or boats used in hauling stones for the foundation of this building. Notwithstanding repeated warnings from the men in charge of the work as to the danger attending this proceeding, the boys continued it until on one occasion one of the front corners of the stone boat struck a tree stump, causing the boat to whirl around with violence. Young Hyatt was thrown from the stone boat, and his foot and ankle were caught between it and a tree stump, injuring him to such an extent that he was laid up for a long time. It was feared he would be crippled for life.

While recovering from this accident, the minister offered to "fit him" for college if he would recite twice a day. He quickly accepted. In the next two years, as he recovered, his interest in a quality education grew. With the assistance of wealthy relatives, he attended Peekskill Academy and then Union College in Schenectady, New York. Upon graduation, he moved to Wilmington to take charge of the Parochial School. He would remain a dominate influence at Delaware Military Academy as well as Pennsylvania Military Academy.

In 1856, at the age of fifteen, Henry Clay Robinett entered DMA. Dr. Clarence R. Moll, former president of Pennsylvania Military College, retells the story of the beginning of military instruction at DMA:

Legend of the school would have it that the introduction to military training came about quite by accident in the fall of 1858 when Principal Hyatt walked into the gymnasium to find his pupils drilling with broomsticks, and at that time he conceived the idea of introducing military training. It is all together possible that the

Hyatt cadets did drill with broomsticks in the fall of 1858, but by plan rather than accident, for Principal Hyatt announced the Infantry Drill and Military Uniform in a circular printed during the summer of 1858 for the term opening September 6, 1858. If the cadets drilled with broomsticks in the fall, it was because the Governor had not yet given the school state arms for drill.[8]

DMA's Birthplace. The adjoining building contained classes and lecture rooms. Courtesy of Buxton, Henry J. Pennsylvania Military College, The Story of One Hundred Years 1821-1921.

Located at 9th and Tatnall Streets in Wilmington, DMA boasted a library of 1,500 volumes by 1859. The curriculum was rigorous: five and a half hours of study each day, three hours of recitation in classes (which averaged about ten students), and two hours for preparation of each classical, math, or scientific lesson. One hour was provided for each lesson in the "primary departments;" boarders, unless members of other churches, attended the Presbyterian Church with a teacher. The school banned tobacco and students spent a portion of each day studying the Scriptures. They also drilled in infantry and sword exercises several times a week. The school year began on the first Monday in September and ended the last Thursday in June. You could be a day student only if your parents or guardians lived in the City of Wilmington [There is no evidence as to whether Henry was a day or resident student though he did live in Wilmington]. Uniform requirements were simple: a coat of cadet grey, single breasted nine buttons in front, four buttons in back and skirt with a "stand up collar to rise no higher than to permit the chin to turn freely over it, to hook in front at the bottom and slope thence up and backward at an angle of 30 degrees on each side." Trousers were made of the same material as the coat and worn throughout the year; "made loose and to spread well over the boots with a black waist let in the outer seam, 1/8 inch in diameter. Their cap was dark blue cloth according to Academy patterns. For undress in summer, each boy could have several suits of strong brown drilling. Overcoats should be made of same dark cloth. Boots or high shoes were always worn on drill." The Uniform was cheap, neat, and serviceable and was worn if on drill and in any public capacity.[9]

A Group of PMA Cadets - 1863 – courtesy of Widener University Archives

Colonel Hyatt instilled loyalty and honor in young cadets while helping to nurture clubs and athletics at the academy.

Both his classical and business courses were very comprehensive and efficient, and his students all of fine character and tone. The Colonel was a man of staunch character and of splendid ability. He was conscientious, earnest and progressive, and always an inspiring and elevating influence upon his students.[10]

Peer groups and social bonds developed based upon wealth, talent, regional affiliations, and at times, the need for mutual protection. The school attempted to maintain as much control as possible with demands for attentiveness to responsibilities, close supervision, and a small student body. Cadets found guilty of rules infractions stayed in on Saturday afternoons and copied scores of words and their definitions from the dictionary. In most such institutions, boys sent their fathers letters concerning conduct and grades. Henry wrote to his father on December 23rd 1857:

Dear Father,
As it was the request of our much beloved Teacher, I will state the studies which I have been pursuing through this last Quarter, my success in them, also my general conduct during the Quarter. My studies have been (1) Latin (2) Chemistry (3) Algebra (4) Composition (5) Penmanship (6) English Grammar. I think as far as I am able to judge that I have succeeded very well in Latin, also in Chemistry. I have improved in Algebra, I have improved very much in Composition; in my writing I have made a great improvement. I have done well in Grammar.

In my general conduct and deportment I believe I have been perfect and conducted myself properly towards my Teacher. This I believe to be a correct statement.
Your Affectionate Son
Henry Clay Robinette

The above is a correct statement, your son has not received a single mark this quarter, he is very gentlemanly in his conduct and most faithful in his studies.
Theo Hyatt[11]

Evidently, as with most military institutions, both then and now, there were conflicts with "townies" as one graduate explained:

The uniform of my day was blue with gold chevrons and a light blue stripe down the trousers. The caps bore the letters 'D. M. A.' for Delaware Military Academy, these being the basis of frequent ructions between the wearers and the 'townies,' who put their own derisive interpretation, 'Delaware Monkey Actors' and 'Dead Men's Artillery,' and hurled these whenever they deemed themselves safe or strong enough, a challenge that the esprit de corps made it imperative to meet, or to cherish for future occasion.[12]

The young men who eventually became the officers and soldiers of the Civil War reflected our national character and were the product of a self-reliant, aggressive, and unsophisticated age. To become a "man" you needed to distinguish yourself by some means. Men of the age admired boldness, the Daniel Boone/Andrew Jackson life-style. Most young men sought self-definition rather than direct confrontation with society and a certain amount of "swagger" and chest thumping was expected. Student life in most academic institutions during this time was often acrimonious; fights and riots were commonplace. Marked by threats, fistfights, duels, and outright brawls, student life was a daily, manly challenge. The code was strong and true: do not appear as if you are afraid of anything or anybody in front of your classmates. One young pugilist at DMA, Harry D. Rust "…came from Tennessee, was one of the best fist fighters in the school, being quick as lightning and extremely scientific. He could rain blows so thick and fast that his opponent was usually licked before he could get started."[13] The boys attempted to organize a cricket team to channel their adolescent energies, but most preferred to play "town ball" (the forerunner of baseball) in their spare time.

As with today, college influences tended to subvert family influence and fatherly control. A student's peers and faculty now held sway. Personal relationships with instructors were important and encouraged. In general, there were two prevailing cultures in student life. The aristocratic planter society cadet looked for authority over his peers that produced a bonding of the elite class and often became a quite violent exercise. The other group, the bit more open-minded middle class sons, built their own values and grew in different ways. Absolute fearlessness and physical courage were special qualities considered obligatory for future officers. You were expected to lead, not drive, your men and "display heroism without indulging in heroics."[14]

Colonel Hyatt's Riders[15] and the State of Delaware

Economically tied to Pennsylvania and in many regards politically tied to the South, Delaware was a divided state with a Southern sense of honor and character and a Northern sense of pragmatism. By 1860, the state boasted a population of 90,589 white inhabitants, 19,829 free persons of color (More free persons of color than any slave holding state save Virginia and Maryland), and 1,798 slaves held by 587 slaveholders.[16] The Delaware Railroad running north/south from Wilmington to Dover divided the state: to the east the Unionists, to the west the pro-slavery faction. Southern Delaware, predominately rural, subsistence farms contrasted with the urban and industrial northern region, centered on Wilmington. The major north/south railroad from New York City to Washington, D.C. and beyond ran through Wilmington, and the city could boast a prosperous seaport as well, resulting in a significant immigrant population boom. In the 1860 Presidential election, 3,815 Delawareans voted for Lincoln, 3,687 for Bell, 1,023 Douglass and 7,347 for the Southern Democrat Breckinridge, clearly a much-divided state with a distinct Southern bent. The name DuPont and the state of Delaware are synonymous

Colonel Theodore Hyatt –
Buxton

even today. the DuPont powder works was the largest provider of explosives in the United States at the time.[17]   Delaware, like other states with strong sentiments on both sides tended to produce many serious issues for families, neighbors, and in this case, the cadets of DMA.[18]

In April of 1859, Delaware Governor Burton appointed Theodore Hyatt Colonel and aide-de-camp on his staff and ordered the issuing of arms to DMA: eighty swords and bayonets, eighty cartridge boxes, fourteen light artillery sabers, forty rifles, and two pieces of field artillery. In the summer, he sent "additional arms."[19] One former cadet said:

Delaware Military Academy had a very high standing. Colonel Theodore Hyatt was a boys' man - all boys honored and respected him. He was a strict disciplinarian during recitations and drills, but when at ease was a charming gentleman with a keen appreciation of all the problems of boydom. He had a sense of humor too, and I will wager that many a time when no one was looking he had a good laugh over some of the pranks that were played in his school.[20]

This caused no small consternation within the pro-South movement in the state.

Hyatt was to have his hands full as politics swirled and war clouds approached. DMA had many cadets from Southern states such as Georgia, Alabama, Tennessee, Kentucky, Louisiana, and Mississippi. James Rush Lincoln, one of Henry's best friends and the only cadet to attend his confirmation at the Holy Trinity (Old Swedes) Church in April of 1860, was born in Frederick County, Maryland four years after Robinett.[21] Lincoln would serve in the 1st Maryland Confederate Cavalry under JEB Stuart. One cadet recalled some of the sectional conflict on campus:

Sectional feeling ran high between the boys, and the space back of the armory was the scene of many fist fights, outside of study hours, between the champions of Northern and Southern policies and principles. These fights usually took place at the noon hour; word would be passed around that a battle of fists was to be staged and the cadets would go to the armory by singles so that the faculty would have no suspicion of what was going on. One of the most spectacular of these fights took place between Levi C. Bird, who later became a noted criminal lawyer of Delaware, and a hot-headed Southerner from Tennessee. During a fierce argument the Southerner called Bird a 'Nigger Lover!' Bird immediately challenged the boy to battle and at noon they met in the armory and fought it out. The fight was terminated when Bird with a well directed right to the jaw knocked out the boy from Tennessee. I remember that it took nearly an hour to bring that lad back to consciousness.[22]

Within a week of the firing on Fort Sumter all the Southern cadets left for Confederate service and numerous Northern cadets joined the Delaware militia units forming in Wilmington and the surrounding area. As graduation approached, DMA held a speech exhibition; Henry spoke on "The Union and the Constitution," James R. Lincoln on "Chivalry," and another close friend, William Irelan on "Labor: improbus omina vincit" [hard work conquers all]. A struggle between Colonel Hyatt and the Secessionist movement over the state issued arms DMA possessed led to an eventual move in the summer of 1862 to West Chester, Pennsylvania. The school was renamed Pennsylvania Military Academy.[23]

Sergeant Major Henry Robinett, Delaware Miltary Academy 1860. His sword is a US M1850 Foot Officers sword and the sword belt has an M1851 Sword belt Plate. (Photo courtesy of Van Hedges)

Endnotes

1. Records of the Office of the Judge Advocate General Court Martial Case Files, 1809-1894; (National Archives Record Group 153, File OO-1898. Robinett quotes from After The Battle, a poem written by Sir Thomas Moore. This project only came about due to a partial research grant from American Military University to which I owe a debt of thanks. I am also deeply indebted to Vonnie Zullos of Horse Soldiers Research. As a fulltime military historian under contract to the U.S. Army, without her numerous trips to the National Archives on my behalf this project would not exist in its current form.

2. Ancestors of Henry Clay Robinett, Robinett Family Association. I am deeply indebted to William Robinette, board member of the Robinett Family Association and database manager, for all his assistance throughout this project. Vice President Joseph Robinette Biden is also a descendent of Allen Robinett. However, according to Biden in a C-Span interview: "It's my Grandmother Biden's maiden name. It's French. And it goes back a long, long way. Allegedly the Robinette's came over with Lafayette and never went home. I don't know that. We can't guarantee that. But it goes back a long way in Maryland and West Virginia" [C-SPAN "Road to the White House" Transcript Date: 09/03/200: http://votesmart.org/speech_detail.php?sc_id=321662&keyword=&phrase= &contain=?q=print] However, William Robinette indicated, "It is true that his grandmother was a Robinette. There are people in France with the name Robinette, however Biden is descended from Allen Robinett and Margaret Symm who came to America in 1682 as part of William Penn's colony. We have never been able to trace the family back to France although it is possible that descendants of Allen came from there (but no proof). The story about Lafayette is a new one to me and again is not true. We know Biden's ancestors. Allen Robinett was the 1st generation in this country in my line. We will probably never know why Allen Robinett purchased land [while still living in London] from William Penn. Allen was not a Quaker." As to why his father named him Henry Clay, we have little evidence. According to William Robinette, "I am not really sure why Henry was given the middle name Clay but I was also thinking that it may have been after Henry Clay. There are 3 other Henry Clay Robinett's that I know of. None are in our HCR's immediate family: 1) Henry Clay Robinett born 1852 and died 1930. 2) Henry Clay Robinette born 1861 and died unknown date. 3) Henry Clay Robinett born 1950." [E-mail from William Robinett Sun 10/4/2009]

3. Military Ancestors of Henry Clay Robinett, Robinett Family Association.

4. U.S. Census Bureau 1860 "Ward 3, New Castle, Delaware; Roll M653_98; Page: 926; Image: 293."

5. Allen was charged with sleeping on post while guarding prisoners at Johnson's Island, Ohio. He was assigned as a ground guard and posted outside of the prison yard at the north-west corner of the prison at the foot of the fence to ensure that prisoners did not escape by digging out or otherwise. He was sentenced as follows: Private, Allen M. Robinett. Company "B," 23rd Pennsylvania Volunteer Infantry, "To be shot to death by musketry, at such time and place as the Commanding General may direct, two-thirds of the members concurring therein. In the case of Private, Allen M. Robinett, Company "B," 23rd Pennsylvania Volunteer Infantry, the proceedings, findings and sentence of the Court are approved. Upon the strong recommendation of the Brigadier-General commanding the Brigade, and the members of the Court, the sentence is remitted. The prisoner will be released from imprisonment and returned to duty."

6. An excellent study on the development of Southern military schools is Rod Andrew's "Long Gray Lines: Southern Military School Tradition, 1839-1915." Chapel Hill, NC: The University of North Carolina Press, 2001. This piece prompted me to wonder why there was so little work on border state military institutions and their influence upon the Civil War. At the Society for Military History Conference in 2007 a paper on 19th Century Military Education by Bradford Wineman, U.S. Army Command and General Staff College, "Citizens, Not Soldiers: Military Service and Antebellum Military Schools" caused me to wonder why DMA was not mentioned and prompted me into looking further at border military institutions. Another interesting study is Jennifer R. Green's "Military Education and the Emerging Middle Class in the Old South." Cambridge, England: Cambridge University Press, 2008.

7. Through the years, DMA has transformed numerous times, changing into Pennsylvania Military Academy, Pennsylvania Military College, PMC Colleges, Widener College, and finally Widener University. A fire at PMA in the 1880s destroyed most of the records for the period. Much of the early information comes to us from: Buxton, Henry J. "Pennsylvania Military College, The Story of One Hundred Years 1821-1921." Chester, PA: 1921 or Moll, Clarence Russell. A "History of Pennsylvania Military College." (Ph.D. diss. New York University, 1954). Buxton cites few sources for verification and Moll at times relies excessively upon Buxton. Those records that survive are located at Widener University Wolfgram Memorial Library Archives. An excellent source on Civil War DMA is an article written by a military history professor of mine at PMC, B. Franklin Cooling III. "Delaware Military Academy, 1859-1862." Delaware History 14, no. 3 (1971). Dr. Cooling has been employed

by the federal government for many years and is presently the Chairman of the Grand Strategy Department at the Industrial College of the Armed Forces at Fort McNair in Washington, D.C. This project would not be complete without noting the outstanding support and assistance provided by Rebecca Warda, PMC Museum curator, Jan Alexander, Reference Librarian and University Archivist, and newly minted 2nd LT Keith Bright, Widener class of 2009. Becky is a kindred spirit in this project and without her efforts on my behalf it would not have been completed. According to Buxton, "President Warren G. Harding in an address at the college in February 1920, said: "If I had a dozen sons I would send every one of them to P. M. C. for here you make men." The occasion of that address was the conferring of the degree of Doctor of Laws upon Mr. Harding. He was then a member of the United States Senate, and when he paid that striking tribute to the college he spoke from firsthand knowledge, for his secretary, Mr. George B. Christian, Jr., is a graduate, Class of 1896. Buxton, 8. "Whatever influence Captain Alden Partridge may have exerted on the foundation of the Delaware Military Academy was in all evidence indirect and related only to his brief associations with the Reverend Corry Chambers who gave his charter to and served on the Board of Trustees of the military academy yet to emerge....Theodore Hyatt, who had adopted the charter from a Partridge School, was himself a disciple of the West Point program and soon adopted it as his yardstick." Moll, 66, 73.

8. Moll, Clarence Russell. "A History of Pennsylvania Military College." (Ph.D. diss. New York University, 1954) The legend of the broom drill is re-enacted annually at every Widener/PMC Homecoming by graduates who put on a broom drill as part of the football half-time program. Buxton (p. 15) claims, "Entering the recreation room of his school one rainy day in the fall of 1858, Theodore Hyatt found his students drilling with broomsticks. The benefits of military instruction dawned up- on the progressive young teacher himself a one-time New York militiaman, and he promptly changed his school into a military academy." Clarence Russell Moll was born on October 31, 1913 in Chalfont, Pennsylvania. He received a bachelor of science in education from Temple University in 1934, followed by a master's degree in education three years later. From 1935 to 1942, Moll taught physics, chemistry, and science at several high schools in New Jersey and Pennsylvania. During World War II, he accepted a position with the U.S. Navy instructing civilian and naval personnel in radio and radar theory. In 1943, Moll left the Navy and joined Pennsylvania Military College as an associate professor of physics and engineering. From 1945 to 1956, he held the various positions of headmaster of the prep school, registrar, and coordinator of engineering. Meanwhile, he earned his Ph.D. in higher education from New York University in 1955. In 1956, Dr. Moll became a vice president before being selected as the first civilian president of Pennsylvania Military College in 1959. Moll retired on June 30, 1981 after

22 years as president. He remained very active in the community, serving as president emeritus and providing advice when called upon. Dr. Moll passed away in December of 2002.
[http://www3.widener.edu/Administration/Office_of_the_President/Institutional_Information/Past_Presidents/Dr_Clarence_R_Moll/4449/]

9. Widener University Archives. "Register of the Graduates and Ex-Cadets of the Pennsylvania Military College That Have Served or Are Now in Service in the Army and Navy of the United States or in the National Guard." And Pennsylvania Military Academy Course Catalogs, 1859 – 1881 Rules and Regulations. Widener University Archives, Chester, PA.

10. Buxton, 21-22.

11. The only surviving letters from Henry, save this one, were written to his brother Theodore "Dorie" and reside at the University of the Pacific: Register of the Robinette Family Papers, 1845-1910, Robinette Family Papers, Mss183, Holt-Atherton Department of Special Collections, University of the Pacific Library. Trisha Pritchard with the Special Collections department was a great help in getting Henry's letters organized.

12. Buxton, 25.

13. Ibid. 23.

14. There are numerous studies of ante-bellum manhood and academic life. The most well known is undoubtedly Bruce Catton's "America Goes to War: The Civil War and Its Meaning in American Culture." Hanover, NH: Wesleyan University Press, 1986. Others include: Rotundo, E. Anthony, "American Manhood: Transformation in Masculinity from the Revolution to the Modern Era." New York: Basic Books, 1993, Pugh, David, "Sons of Liberty: The Masculine Mind in Nineteenth-century America." Westport, CT: Greenwood Press, 1983, Wakelyn, Jon L. "Antebellum College Life and the Relations between Fathers and Sons." In "The Web of Southern Social Relations: Women, Family, and Education," edited by J. Fraser Jr., R. Frank Saunders Jr., and Jon Wakelyn, Athens: University of Georgia Press, 1985, and Kett, Joseph F. "Rites of Passages: Adolescence in America, 1790 to the Present." New York: Basic Books, 1977.

15. As cadet at PMC, we quite often sang about Colonel Hyatt's Riders while running in formation - "We are Colonel Hyatt's Riders, we are riders of the night..."

16. University of Virginia Census Browser. http://fisher.lib.virginia.edu/collections/stats/histcensus/

17. Thomas J. Reed, and W. Andrew McKay, along with Reverend Anthony R. Wade wrote the best study of Delaware during this period, "Untying the Political Knot: Delaware During the War Between the States." Wilmington, NC: Broadfoot Publishing Co., 2001. In it, they recount an episode on the 18th of April, 1861 when "two men dressed in women's clothing were apprehended at the Du Pont Powder co. works on the Brandywine. President Henry DuPont was thoroughly alarmed that secessionists intended to blow up his powder works. He obtained Pennsylvania militia to guard the powder works, since Delaware had not yet called up its militia." p. 16.

18. Pearson, Alden B., Jr., 'Middle-class, Border-state Family during the Civil War' in "The Southern Common People: Studies in Nineteenth-century Social History," edited by Edward Magdol and Jon L. Wakelyn. Westport, CT: Greenwood Press, 1980, is a good study of the effects on the war upon families from Border States.

19. B. Franklin Cooling III. "Delaware Military Academy, 1859-1862." Delaware History 14, no. 3 (1971).

20. Buxton, 25.

21. Holy Trinity Church Records, Wilmington 1800-1860 Vol. 1 page 75. Special thanks to Raymond Nichols, volunteer at the church archives and Rebecca L. Wilson, Executive Director of the Old Swedes Foundation. The Holy Trinity Church was the center of religious life in Wilmington for much of its existence. The church was built in 1698 over the original graveyard. The church was established as a Swedish Lutheran Church and the church building was constructed in 1698-1699. The church was placed under the jurisdiction of the Protestant Episcopal Church in 1791. It flourishes today as the nation's oldest church building still standing as originally built. It is still in regular use for worship." Many prominent families of Wilmington and the surrounding area were members including Robinett's fiancé's. Henry was confirmed and baptized in April 1860 just before his graduation from DMA at the age of nineteen. According to Dr. John Brinsfield, historian for the U.S. Army Chaplains Corps it was not unusual to be confirmed and baptized at the age of 19-22. James R. Lincoln will serve in the 1st Maryland Cavalry (CSA) under J.E.B. Stuart during the war and after the war move to Iowa where he became superintendent of a coal mining company in Boone, Iowa and the town's mayor. He went to Iowa State College (University) in 1883 and served as the Professor of Military Tactics until 1919. Lincoln also held the positions of Steward of the College

(1883) and Professor of Mining Engineering (1892-1898). Soon after coming to Iowa, Lincoln joined the Iowa National Guard and held commissions as Captain, Major, Lieutenant Colonel, Colonel, Inspector General, and Brigadier General. During the Spanish American War, he mobilized Iowa's troops and went to the front. Unable to serve actively in World War I, Lincoln remained at Iowa State training others for active duty. He passed away August 4, 1922 in Ames, Iowa. James Rush Lincoln Papers, RS 13/16/13, University Archives, Special Collections Department, Iowa State University Library. Special thanks to Michelle Christian, Assoc. Professor and University Records Analyst at Iowa State for her assistance.

22. Buxton, 26.

23. In January of 1861 Colonel Hyatt said, "I am sick of the matter, [if] I have to lose the arms, I may as well do it at once, the thing is seriously injuring my school, as it keeps me so much out of it" [John Dale to Thomas F. Bayard 29 JAN 1861, Bayard Papers, Delaware Historical Society.] Bayard replied, "We can take care in [Gov.] Burton's time that he [Hyatt] gets no more [arms]. A cord wood stick mounted will do him as well, if he is no better at shooting than he is at teaching." [13 FEB 1861, Bayard Papers]

Chapter II:
Duty and Honor

After graduation, Robinett's ambition would not allow him to settle for a commission in the Delaware volunteers. He wrote his brother, Theodore:

Perhaps I should have told you before, I went personally to the Secretary of War [Simon Cameron] and obtained my appointment. I could, I suppose as well have gotten a 1st Lieutenant as a 2nd but I preferred the later in consideration of age etc, etc. I belong to the 1st Infantry Company C.[1]

When referring to his choice of a Regular Army commission over the Delaware volunteers that many of his peers joined Henry wrote, "I have followed my own inclinations, not their advice." His desire for fame and reward began to show. Commissioned a Second Lieutenant in August of 1861 just a few weeks after graduation, Robinett was looking for a career path that would bring him the recognition and acknowledgement.

Henry joined the 1st U.S. Infantry on September 28th.[2] The regiment, stationed in Missouri, had previously participated in Wilson's Creek, and possessed a reputation as a solid, effective unit.[3] Initially stationed at Leavenworth, Kansas, Henry was shortly assigned to St. Joseph, Missouri. Proud of his assignment, and with a strong sense of self, honor, and purpose, he wrote in rather fractured English:

Truly it is as I direct this letter to you from one (formerly) of Secessiondom's strongholds. I am here transacting business for no less a personage than Uncle Samuel. I suppose I can safely say that

I am now a part and parcel of his estate. My Quarters are two fine spacious rooms with the addition of a smaller one in the rear of a new Cottage house of the handsomest finish. I am well pleased with my position and the duties devolving upon me in consequence of holding it. I am in sole command of my company and My Capt. W.E. Prince is Commanding Officer of the Fort. My company, I commanding, (is) had, under the directing of the Officer in Charge of the works, the honor of stricking the first spade and felling the first tree. Our duties (2nd Lieut) in the Garrison consist of the following, attendance at Reveille (Sun rise) Retreat (Sun set) at which time the company appear under arms and Tattoo (8 1/2 o'clock night). We also work in the trenches (supretend of course, we never could suffer the indignity of being compelled to work) with our company.[4]

Fort Smith (23BN71) is situated slightly to the north and west of St. Joseph, Missouri. The fort was constructed in 1861 by the Union troops under Colonel Smith who commanded troops of the 16th and 52nd Illinois infantry. (St. Louis Community College. Professor Michael J. Fuller Professor of Anthropology: http://users.stlcc.edu/mfuller/Fortsmith.html)

While stationed in Missouri, Henry was responsible for the processing of paroled Union soldiers. Sergeants Edwin Craig, William Geeslin, and P.C. Causey along with 107 other men of the 3rd Regiment Missouri Volunteers taken prisoner on the 20th of September, described the event to General J. W. Davidson:

> *We signed no parole and were not paroled to be exchanged (as our officers have represented). We then went to our homes. Shortly afterwards our officers were released and came to Saint Joseph (where the regiment was organized), and ordered us all to report there to be paid off and discharged. On the 26th of October, 1861, we were mustered out of service by Lieutenant Robinett, U.S. Army, mustering officer, and received our discharges. We would also state, in addition to the above statement, that we were put on duty on our return to the regiment and not sworn in or regularly mustered in again.*[5]

On November 23, 1861 Henry was promoted to First Lieutenant and his career seemed to be on the course he plotted.

The spring of 1862 found Robinett taking part in a few small engagements. In March, his company was independently assigned during the siege of New Madrid, Missouri where they manned siege artillery rather than performing the traditional functions of infantry. This was, no doubt, his second experience with artillery pieces, as DMA possessed two pieces presented by the governor of Delaware, caliber unknown. After New Madrid, Union forces pushed down the Mississippi River's western bank and constructed batteries near Ruddle's Point opposite Tiptonville, Tennessee. The 1st U.S. possessed a collection of siege guns: two 20-pounder Parrotts, four 30-pounder Parrotts, and four 24-pounder siege pieces.[6] Robinett would later put these large siege guns to good use.

The 2nd Texas Infantry

Robinett's experiences in the Civil War were twice inexorably tied to that of the 2nd Texas Infantry Regiment. In April of 1862, as Confederate General P.T.G. Beauregard was developing the defenses around Corinth that would assume his name, the 2nd Texas Infantry arrived from the Houston/Galveston area on its way to Shiloh. Their uniforms of white wool caused one Yankee prisoner to describe them as "hell-cats that went into battle dressed in their grave clothes." One veteran of the 2nd Texas who participated in the Battle of Shiloh remarked in a letter home,

I have one thing to say--I thought the Yankees are better fighters than they are. I can assure you that every time our regiment got after them they run. They could not stand the cold steel. At one time, our boys run three thousand of them.[7]

On April 6, 1862, their first day at Shiloh, the unit helped complete the encirclement of the Hornet's Nest and dined on Union stores that night. The following morning Colonel John Creed Moore, the original commander, received a battlefield promotion and turned command over to Lieutenant Colonel William Peleg Rogers who would lead them throughout the rest of the battle.[8]

When they [2nd Texas] were ordered to charge a battery Monday morning, they were ordered to charge upon an open field, and while charging were ordered to halt [without firing], and received a murderous fire from the enemy lying in ambush. Our loss in ten minutes was greater than the whole of Sunday.[9]

General William J. Hardee wrote this report of the incident:

Many of our best regiments, signalized in the battle of Shiloh by their steady valor, reeled under sanguinary struggle on the succeeding day. In one instance, that of the Second Texas regiment, commanded by Colonel Moore, the men seemed appalled, fled

from the field without apparent cause, and were so dismayed that my efforts to rally them were unavailing....I was about the same distance (40 yards) from it when it commenced firing; and apparently before half the pieces of the regiment were discharged it broke and fled disgracefully from the field. I sent Captain Clare, then acting on my staff, to pursue and rally the regiment. He afterward informed me that it could not be rallied; that a portion of the regiment swore they would not return to the field, and when told that I would call them a 'pack of cowards,' said they did not care a damn what I might call them.[10]

In reality, the unit had been ordered to advance without proper skirmishers forward and during the advance, their superior chain of command became muddled. Hardee's staff gave direct orders to the troops the consequence of which, while under fire, caused widespread confusion in the ranks. Hardee's staff did not know the location of General Breckinridge's troops and used poor judgment in ordering the men to hold their fire. This slanderous account by Hardee haunted the 2nd Texas throughout the remainder of their time in the war and significantly contributed to the wrath Robinett and the 1st U.S. Infantry would feel from the 2nd Texas Infantry. Colonel Rogers described the events:

The gallantry of our Reg, is spoken of by all. Our charges were magnificent. The last charge on Sunday evening and two on Monday were truly grand. Those I lead in person, am commanding carrying our battle flag. It has six holes through it one in the staff- my horse slightly wounded in the shoulder. I received a blow from a limb cut off by a cannon ball.[11]

After falling back and regrouping, the 2nd Texas took to the field and attacked, the Yankee units retreated and Rogers pursued them for half a mile. The Texans were too exhausted to stand against Buell's fresh troops that arrived to reinforce Grant and slowly pulled back along with the entire Rebel line.[12] The people of Houston had heard rumors of the regiment's cowardice and Rogers could not let that stand. By the time the 2nd Texas once again reappeared in front of Corinth they were spoiling for a fight to regain their questioned honor and reputation. Unknown to Robinett and Colonel Rogers, there were fated to meet in the coming months.

The Crossroads of the Confederacy

After Shiloh on May 2, 1862 Robinett, according to his own writings, participated in an engagement at "Purdy Bridge."[13] He is mistaken. Henry is probably referring to activities related to movements conducted by Pope's army on May 3, 1862, in which Paine's division made a reconnaissance south by west to Farmington, descending into the swamp (north) of Seven Mile Creek. A brisk skirmishing attended this advance. The bridge across Seven Mile Creek was found destroyed and the road beyond obstructed with fallen timber. The Federals repaired the bridge and continued toward Farmington, where they again clashed with Confederates. After an hour's exchange of fire, the Confederates fell back approximately two miles, "the road being covered with cast-off clothing, canteens, blankets, haversacks, arms, and accouterments."[14] Paine advanced south into Farmington, before being recalled. The Union forces re-crossed the creek and encamped one and one-half miles north of it, on Chambers Creek, leaving a sufficient force in the swamp to guard the bridge and road, linking Farmington with Hamburg. This is the only activity, other than cavalry, that involves any portion of the army around May 2. The area north and east of Farmington is extremely swampy, with a series of smaller creeks that empty into the main artery. Pope's advance passed through a considerable portion of this area. There is a chance Robinett simply made an error concerning the identity of the bridge in question, the primary structure being on the Hamburg-Farmington road at Seven Mile Creek, which traversed the wide drainage via a causeway either side of the bridge. The other possibility is that Robinett may have indeed encountered another bridge on a road leading north from Farmington, which he presumed linked the community with Purdy.[15]

A few days later, on May 15, 1862, Robinett and the 1st U.S. Infantry found themselves in front of the Confederate fortifications at Corinth where their siege guns were used to some effect "doing considerable execution."[16] On May 30, the Confederate forces withdrew, and the battery "took station there." At this point in his career, Robinett was now well versed in the finer points of siege artillery as well as the environs of Corinth that would serve him well in just a few short months. Unbeknownst to him, as his men prepared their fortifications, the position they constructed would change his life in a dramatic fashion and become the fulcrum of a Rebel assault on Corinth. General Henry W. Halleck ordered a defensive line of artillery redoubts constructed to protect Corinth from the west and south. During the summer, the Union forces constructed seven redoubts approximately one and a half miles from and surrounding the entire city. In September, Grant relocated his headquarters to Jackson, Mississippi leaving General William Rosecrans in command of the forces in and around Corinth. Rosecrans decided it was too hard to occupy the complete "Halleck Line" and built five redoubts closer to town. He issued orders to connect the "Rosecrans Line" earthworks with lines of breastworks and strengthened them with abatis[17] 400 yards in front of each fortification. According to *Battles and Leaders*, the Union Forces employed Black contrabands in twenty-five man squads to help build their fortifications.[18]

Corinth was a young town, incorporated in 1856, with the completion of the Memphis and Charleston Railroad the following year. By 1861, the Mobile and Ohio Railroad had come through town thus creating the "Crossroads of the Confederacy" where no less than six key roads also meet.[19] This initiated its economic and strategic importance. The city was, quite possibly, second only to Richmond in this regard. The town was astride two strategic invasion routes into the Deep South, the Mississippi Valley to Vicksburg and Chattanooga to Atlanta making it a key line of communications node and supply depot. The 1,200 to

1,500 Mississippians who lived in Corinth trod earthen lanes, surrounded by low, rolling hills covered with a dense forest of red and white oak and pine. Much of the area was dismal swamp land often causing a dank, moist odor to float over the town with an ever-present threat of malaria. Little fresh water existed and what did was often milky-white with a rancid taste. During the summer

Downtown Corinth - Harper's Weekly June 21, 1862

and early fall the heat could be quite stifling. The summer of 1862 saw a drought in northern Mississippi, and most of the wells ran dry.[20]

The six companies of the 1st U. S. consisting of siege artillery under Capt. G. A. Williams were unattached within the Army of the Mississippi, Robinett commanding Company C. The entrenched Battery Robinett was located 675 yards west of town and boasted three twenty-pound Parrotts, one facing northeast, one north, and one northwest. An earthen lunette with a high parapet and a ten-foot ditch faced the west and north with embrasure for the guns and an opening to the rear.[21] In most field fortifications, a lunette consisted of a detached field work open in the rear with two faces forming a salient angle and two flanks adjoining the faces in a roughly "V" shape. They were usually employed as forward works within a line.[22] Extending from the lunette to the railroad was a covered way providing protected access to the position. Battery Williams, commanded by Robinett's commander, was to Robinett's east and rear with three thirty-pound Parrots and one 8-inch siege howitzer.

As Robinett and his men prepared their position, the 2nd Texas saw its next formal combat at Iuka, Mississippi, on 19

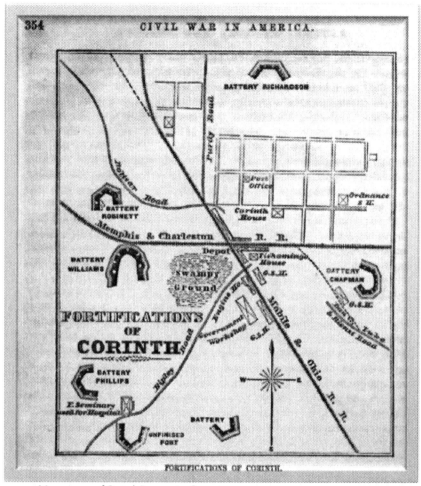

Map courtesy of Corinth Interpretive Center

September where it was cited for bravery, only the prelude for its return to honor. Marching with Major General Sterling Price's Army of the West from Iuka, they rendezvoused with Major General Earl Van Dorn's Army of West Tennessee, as the combined force was also called by Van Dorn, and marched to the northwest of Corinth. October 3 dawned with a 5:56 sunrise, and by noon, the temperature soared to 94 degrees - unusually hot for October in northern Mississippi. At 10 A.M., the Rebel forces were but three miles northwest of Corinth. General Rosecrans forces advanced into the old Rebel entrenchments northwest of town. Around 10 A.M. Major General Van Dorn's attack began. His initial plan was a double envelopment but rapidly evolved into a frontal assault as Union forces withdrew from the outer perimeter. The 2nd Texas, heavily engaged most of the morning, charged across 300 yards of open ground to take a series of rifle pits, regrouped and charged again, splitting the 7th Illinois in two. General William Rosecrans' men of the Army of The Tennessee "did not act or fight well" yet he wrote, "I think we shall handle them. We are at the outer line of works."[23]

Endnotes

1. Henry Robinette Letter to Theodore Robinett, October 24, 1861. Register of the Robinette Family Papers, 1845-1910, Robinette Family Papers, Mss183, Holt-Atherton Department of Special Collections, University of the Pacific Library.

2. According to the September 2, 1861 DMA Circular, Robinett was a member of the Board of Instruction as an Assistant Acting Instructor. There is no evidence he took up the post as he was already joining the 1st U.S. Infantry. The DMA Circular indicates that his grades were excellent and that Colonel Hyatt held him in high regard.

3. "The five companies of the regiment in the Indian Territory at the outbreak of the war,—B, C, D, E and F,—marched to Fort Leavenworth, reaching that post May 31, 1861, under the command of Lieutenant Colonel W. H. Emory, who had been directed (April 17) to collect all the troops in the Indian Territory and take them to that station. This battalion was present at the battle of Wilson's Creek, Mo., August 10, 1861, losing 80 officers and men killed, wounded and missing." Theophilus Francis Rodenbough, William L Haskin eds. "The Army of the United States, Historical Sketches of Staff and Line with Portraits of Generals-in-Chief." (New York: Maynard, Merrill, & Co. 1896) 407.

4. Ibid. Note Robinett's disdain for an officer "suffering the indignity" of working alongside his men.

5. OR--SERIES II--VOLUME IV [S# 117] p. 557 Evidently at Shiloh prisoners from this regiment were "roughly treated" by Confederate forces questioning them about their pervious exchange.

6. Rodenbough, 408.

7. The best study of the 2nd Texas was written by Joseph E Chance, "The Second Texas Infantry: From Shiloh to Vicksburg." Austin, Texas: Eakin Press, 1984. This unit played a significant role on both the successes of Henry Robinett and his ultimate failure and will cross paths with Robinett and his 1st US Infantry twice at both Corinth and Vicksburg where the 2nd Texas would ultimately surrender. The Yankee prisoner's account can be found in Gen. J. C. Moore, "Some Confederate War Incidents," Confederate Veteran, Volume XII, March, 1904. Sam Houston Jr. was a private in the 2nd Texas and at Shiloh discovered his Bible had a bullet hole in the back cover through the New Testament to Psalm 40 "Make haste, O God, to deliver me: make haste to help me, O Lord."

8. http://www.tshaonline.org/handbook/online/articles/RR/fro64.html accessed 7 July 2009.] William P. Rogers was raised on a plantation in Aberdeen, MS. Studied medicine and graduated at 21 then abandoned his practice to study law. He served in the Mexican War with Co. K (Tombigbee Guards) 1st Miss. Reg. (Mississippi Rifles) commanded by Col. Jeff Davis. [Handbook of Texas Online. Rogers, William Peleg] According to Cozzens, Rogers and Davis had a deep seated animosity that almost led to a duel during the Mexican War that Zachary Taylor prevented. [Cozzens 254] Rogers gained a reputation for bravery during the capture of Monterrey with Gen. Zachary Taylor watching. President Taylor appointed Rogers US Consul in Vera Cruz for four years. He later settled in Texas in 1851 at Washington-on-the Brazos, then Houston in 1859. Rogers was a cousin of Sam Houston's wife and a close personal friend. He felt secession was not right but felt deep loyalty to the South. Davis offered him command of 1st TX Inf. in VA which he rejected preferring to help defend Texas and accepted a junior command in 2nd TX. Davis held a deep-seated grudge for his rejection and refused to promote Rogers despite numerous recommendations to do so. [Chance]

9. Christian, William Capt. "Captain William Christian of Company A on the battle of Shiloh." Tri-Weekly Telegraph. Houston, Texas, July 4, 1862.

10. Chance, 36-37.

11. Labuzan, Charles C. 1st Lt. Letter. Greenville Dodge Papers, Iowa State Historical Library. The unit received 33% casualities of which 10% were killed. Sam Houston, Jr, seriously wounded, found by Yankees, when Bible revealed who he was and was saved by chaplain-that had met his father when he was a U.S. Senator.

12. Col. Rogers received news on the 19th of June that individuals in Houston were spreading rumors about regiment and was deeply upset by the news. He sent letters to the editor of the Tri-Weekly Telegraph defending the actions of the

2nd Texas. Rogers is convinced he must prove the bravery of the regiment--and he will at Corinth.

13. Records of the Office of the Judge Advocate General Court Martial Case Files, 1809-1894; (National Archives Record Group 153, File OO-1898). This is the transcript of Court Martial #3 of Robinett.

14. O.R. Series I, X, pt. I, 714-715, 801-802.

15. There are only three references to a Purdy Bridge near Shiloh found in the ORs., none of which indicate any engagements and only detailing the assignment of pickets to the bridge. "On the 4th of May the reserves were moved forward by me, the Third Division from their position near the Pittsburg and Purdy Bridge across Owl Creek to Mickey's White House, and the First Division, under command of Brigadier-General Judah, to the vicinity of Monterey." SERIES I--VOLUME X/1 [S# 10], p. 754.; "The First Brigade will keep a strong guard at the Purdy Bridge, over Owl Creek, with pickets extending forward as far as prudence will admit." SERIES I--VOLUME X/2 [S# 11], p. 102-3.; and "That in accomplishing this purpose two regiments have been detached from the First (General Logan), one of which is encamped at the Pittsburg and Crump's Landing Bridge, and the other at the Pittsburg and Purdy Bridge...Similar pickets are kept up by the Third Division (General Wallace), to guard the line of Owl Creek from a point near the Pittsburg and Purdy bridge to a point west of Monterey." SERIES I--VOLUME X/2 [S# 11], p. 1932-3. According to Stacy D. Allen, "Pope acknowledged the May 3rd activity in a report cited above [OR, I, X, pt. I, pp. 801-802]. He was big on citing the activities of his army, and it is my impression had any portion of his army been engaged on May 2nd, he would have acknowledged it as he did with that of May 3rd.

16. The 1st Infantry was unattached within the army organization at this time and was most likely the six companies (or part thereof) were temporarily attached to Paine's division for the advance on May 3rd. They are not documented to have participated in the published Official Records--but this lack thereof is not uncommon for organizations (Union or Confederate) participating in the advance upon and siege of Corinth. The Confederate force on May 3rd, based on correspondence in OR, I, X, pt. 2, pp. 485-486, appears to have been advanced elements of Hardee's corps, most likely troops from Cleburne's brigade."

17. Rodenbough, 408.

18. "An abatis is an obstacle composed of felled trees stripped of their leaves and smaller branches with remaining large branches sharpened into points. Trees were placed side by side and staked down with the sharpened branches

31

pointing toward approaches to the protected field work. Usually positioned on the engaged side of field works within close musket range of the parapet. Its purpose, like other obstacles exterior to the ditch, was to break an assaulting body of troops' momentum and hold them up under close musket fire delivered from the parapet." P.E. McDuffie, ed. "Civil War Field Fortifications Digital Research Library," October, 1997 - December, 2008, http://civilwarfortifications.com/dictionary/xga-001.html

19. Johnson, Robert Underwood. "Battles and Leaders of the Civil War" VOL II. New York : The Century Co., 1887-1888, p. 741.

20. One of the most definitive works on the role of Corinth during the Civil War is Stacy D. Allen's "Crossroads of the Western Confederacy" Blue & Gray Magazine Visitor's Guide-Corinth Mississippi, 2007. Allen is Chief Ranger Shiloh National Military Park and an expert on all matters Shiloh and Corinth. Tom Parson, Park Ranger at The Corinth Civil War Interpretive Center, a part of the Shiloh Park is also an invaluable resource. I deeply appreciate Tom's assistance in my examination of Robinett and his role at Corinth. The Yankee prisoner's account can be found in: Moore, J. C. Gen. "Some Confederate War Incidents," Confederate Veteran, Volume XII, March, 1904.

21. A short work on the battle of Corinth is Steven Nathaniel Dossman's, "Campaign for Corinth: Blood in Mississippi." Abilene, TX: McWhiney Foundation Press, 2006.

22. Another good work on the Battle of Corinth is Peter Cozzens', "The Darkest Days of the War: The Battles of Iuka & Corinth." Chapel Hill: University of North Carolina Press, 1997. For an excellent study of field fortifications see Hess, Earl J. "Field Armies and Fortifications in the Civil War." Chapel Hill, North Carolina: University of North Carolina Press, 2005.

23. McDuffie, http://civilwarfortifications.com/dictionary/xgl-003.html.
U.S. War Department. A Compilation of the Official Record of the Union and Confederate Armies. Washington: GPO, 1880-1901. Series I--Volume XVII/1 [S# 24] p. 160. Hereafter referred to as OR.

Chapter III:
Desperate in the Extreme:
The Battle of Corinth

During the first day at Corinth, Battery Robinett played little role, firing a few rounds at the end of the day. As the day's fight ended, Captain Williams noted:

> *As there were indications of the enemy reforming, Lieutenant Robinett, who commanded the battery, threw a few shells among them, to which they replied with four shots from their artillery; but night coming on the firing ceased.*[1]

The Confederate forces, just a few hundred yards from Corinth and exhausted from the day's heat and fight, sought to reorganize and prepare for the following day. Van Dorn ordered a dawn attack to take the town. In a telegram to Richmond, he wrote:

> *We have driven the enemy from every position. We are within three-quarters of a mile of Corinth. The enemy are huddled together about the town, trying to hold the position. Our loss, I am afraid, is heavy. It is near night. Lovell's and Price's troops have our thanks.*[2]

Van Dorn was risking his entire command in order to take the vital crossroads.

During the evening, near 9 P.M., the Union troops were reinforced by Fuller's "Ohio Brigade," Stanley's 2nd Division, Army of the Mississippi. Fuller deployed Colonel Joseph Lee Kirby Smith's 43rd Ohio in breastworks near the crest of a small ridge on the left of Battery Robinett. The 63rd Ohio, under Colonel John W. Sprague, deployed on Robinett's right without benefit of breastworks with Major Zephaniah S. Spaulding's 27th Ohio, and Colonel A. W. Gilbert's 39th Ohio, commanding, further to the right towards the Mobile and Ohio Railroad, the Unionist 11th Missouri from Colonel Joseph A. Mower's, 2nd Brigade was positioned directly behind Robinett's battery.

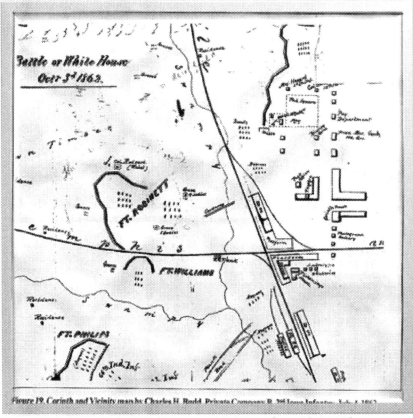

Map by Private Charles H. Budd Company B, 2nd Iowa Infantry, July 4, 1863[3]

Under a full moon, the temperatures plummeted. No fires were permitted. While skirmishers on both sides exchanged occasional shots, Samuel Byers of the 5th Iowa wrote:

All the night we lay under the brightest moon I ever saw. Under the same moonlight, and only 600 yards away from us, also lay the victorious rebel army. They believed Corinth as good as taken but they had only taken our outer line of forts. Yet it looked bad for us....out there lay thousands of others in line, only waiting the daylight to be also mangled and torn.[4]

Van Dorn considered an attack under the full moon but rejected the idea since the men appeared too worn and Yankee emplacements too difficult to see clearly. Still mindful of the accusations at Shiloh and a perceived slight by Davis failing to promote him, Colonel Rogers remarked to Captain McGinnis, "Tomorrow Jeff Davis must allow my promotion, or tomorrow I die."

The morning of October 4 dawned cold, chilling the soldiers (September had been unseasonably warm), few of whom slept much during the night. In the early hours, Confederate batteries moved into position for the 4 A.M. pre-assault bombardment. Meanwhile Rosecrans, busy most of the night re-shuffling his troops, finally lay down at 3 A.M. to try to catch a few hours of rest before the impending attack. His slumber was interrupted at 4 A.M. by the intense Rebel artillery barrage and he was back in the saddle by 4:30. A soldier in Fuller's Brigade noted:

With the earliest dawn of day, the enemy's battery in front opened its fire. What a magnificent display! Nothing we had ever seen looked like the flashes of those guns. No rockets ever scattered fire like the bursting of those shells![5]

At the same time, Colonel Rogers, essentially acting as a brigadier general, donned an armored vest and pinned a note to his clothing with his name, age, rank, command, and the address of friends.[6] Roger's objective for the 2nd Texas, along with the 6th and 9th Texas, the 35th Mississippi, and the 42nd Alabama attached to him, was Battery Robinett. His force amounted to perhaps seven to eight hundred men, a "handful of dauntless men" according to Monroe F. Cockrell's *The Lost Account of the Battle of Corinth.*[7]

The barrage continued for almost an hour yet Robinett's guns remained silent. "Lieutenant Robinette did not respond for some twenty minutes; in the meantime, training his guns to the point of attack so as not to send one useless shot."[8] He and Captain Williams were awaiting dawn to reveal the precise source of the fire. The night before, a Union field battery had set up between the two positions and they were fearful of striking their comrades in the low pre-dawn light.[9] As dawn approached, the guns of both batteries opened, J.S. McKinstry, one of Colonel Rogers' men, later wrote:

We were discovered at dawn, and Forts Williams, Robinette, and College Hill opened a terrific enfilade fire of shot and shell upon us. We lay flat upon our faces and the shells passed a few feet over us (we thought these feet were only inches), doing but slight damage.[10]

With enough light to determine the source of enemy fire, Robinett opened in conjunction with Batteries Williams and Phillips. "After Lieut. Robinette opened his battery of Parrot guns the scene soon changed - as only a few shots were necessary to drive the Rebels from their position."[11]

The cannonading was heavy for an hour and a half. Our regiment lay down close and stood it nobly. The shells flew thick and fast cutting off large limbs and filling the air with fragments many burst within twenty feet and the pieces passed within two or three. It was extremely unpleasant and I prayed for forgiveness of my sins and made up my mind to go through.[12]

Forced to cease-fire within thirty minutes, Hoxton's Tennessee battery from Brig.-Gen. Dabney H. Maury's division attempted to limber and withdraw. Fired upon and overrun by skirmishers from the 63rd Ohio, they abandoned a gun. A few of Robinett's men moved forward and with assistance returned with the James gun, caisson, and five rebel artillerymen.[13] Meanwhile the 2nd Texas halted the advance of Stanley's skirmishers while still taking heavy fire from Robinett.

By 6 A.M., the field fell silent, and the sun rose to a clear and cloudless sky. The Confederate attack did not step off as planned, and Van Dorn sent staff officers to determine why. By 7 A.M., still no attack had commenced. By 8 A.M., Rosecrans too was wondering why no attack had followed the furious barrage and ordered General Stanley to determine why by posting skirmishers to his front and "feeling the enemy." Meanwhile, CSA Brigadier General Louis Hébert notified Van Dorn that he had fallen ill and could not lead his division in the attack. Brigadier General Martin E. Green assumed command at once, and he was ordered to begin the advance. Another two hours would pass before he was sufficiently organized to attack.

Finally, at 10 A.M., the left flank of the Confederate forces stepped off towards Battery Powell, Union position on the right, well to Robinett's east. Just afterwards Cozens recounts the description of events as told by Captain Oscar Jackson, 63rd Ohio:

In a few minutes the left went into action in splendid state at 10 1/4 o'clock Col Rogers came up by us only saying "Alabama forces" … unmindful of shell of shot and moved forward.…We were now met by a perfect storm of grape canister and cannon balls and minie balls. Oh God I have never seen the like the men fell like grass even here giving out one tremendous cheer we dashed to the bottom of the hill on which the fortifications are situated.[14]

Private J.A. McKinstry of the 42nd Alabama remembered: "We remained in this position, hugging the ground, for four mortal hours before the signal gun was fired and the order to charge was given. The forts caught the sound of the signal gun, and ceased firing. We raised the rebel yell, and made a rush for the opening, some fifty yards in our front."[15] Once out of the woods and formed, Rogers men moved forward without the benefit of the traditional "Rebel yell." Jackson continues his account:

In my campaigning I had never seen anything so hard to stand as that slow, steady tramp. Not a sound was heard, but they looked as if they intended to walk over us. I afterwards stood a bayonet charge when the enemy came at us on the double-quick with a yell and it was not so trying on the nerves as that steady, solemn advance. I could see that my men were affected by it.[16]

Major Sam Byers recalled the moment's amazement and the 5th Iowa's reaction:

Suddenly we heard something, almost like a great whirlwind.... amazed to see a great black column, ten thousand strong, moving like a might storm-cloud out of the woods and attacking the troops and forts to our left. Instantly we changed direction a little and, without further firing, witnessed one of the greatest assaults of any war. It was the storming of Fort Robinett.... These recklessly advanced on the forts, climbing over the tress and bending their heads against the awful storm of grape and canister from all our cannon....Even an enemy could feel pity to see brave men so cruelly slaughtered.[17]

Battery Robinett was about to become the focal point for Rebel wrath, with much of the hopes for a Union victory riding on the events whirling around Robinett, his three 20-pounders, and his infantry support. Smith ordered the 43rd Ohio to half wheel and the left company face north to repel the impending Confederate attack. Robinett awaited Colonel Rogers and the Rebel charge as they moved into the abatis to his front. It was painfully obvious to the Texans that Robinett knew how to fight his guns; Private McKinstry remembered:

In front of us was the most obstructive abattis[18] *that it was my misfortune to encounter ...the forts (belched) destruction into our ranks; yet our men did not waver or halt ... when about half through the abattis, Robinett changed shells for grape and canister on us. Our yells grew fainter and our men fell faster, but at last we reached the unobstructed ground in front of the fort. Going had fallen with a bullet in his leg. Comrade Crawford, of Company*

A, dropped his gun, and, almost before the flag had touched the dust, hoisted it again, and shouted: "On to the fort, boys!" A few steps farther, and the guns of the fort again changed their charges; now whole bags of buckshot were being belched from the cannons'

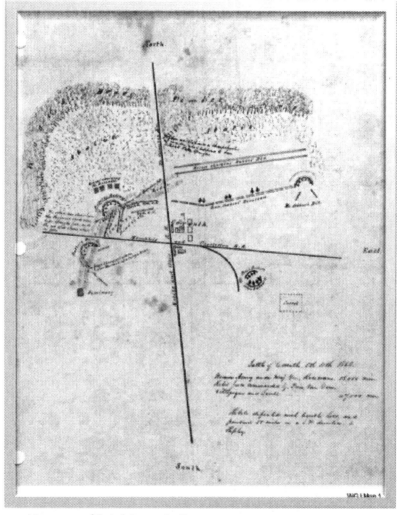

Map courtesy of Corinth Interpretive Center

mouths into our now nearly annihilated ranks, and our flag went down the ill-fated third time to rise no more on that battlefield.[19]

The Rebel columns shudder and after clearing the abatis, paused to reform. Colonel Rogers then gave the order to charge. By this point, smoke covered the battlefield and the Rebels were only fifty yards from their prize, Battery Robinett.[20]

Captain Oscar L. Jackson of the 63rd Ohio noted, "As the smoke cleared away, there was apparently ten yards square of a mass of struggling bodies and butternut clothes. Their column appeared to reel like a rope shaken at the end."[21] Thomas Hagan of the 2nd Texas remembered:

We advanced through open hilly ground on which there was not a single bush to screen a person from the terrible storm of shot and shell from their heavy siege guns which were in full view for over a mile [exaggeration], and looked like if [sic] hell had been let loose. Shells bursting all around you; round shot plowing down the hill almost by the bushel; it is a miracle how anyone escaped.[22]

In the report Captain Williams prepared detailing the fight at Robinett he noted:

During the time the enemy were being repulsed from the town my attention was drawn to the left side of the battery by the firing from Battery Robinett, where I saw a column advancing to storm it. After advancing a short distance they were repulsed, but immediately reformed, and, storming the work, gained the ditch, but were repulsed. During this charge 8 of the enemy, having placed a handkerchief on a bayonet and calling to the men in the battery not to shoot them, surrendered, and were allowed to come into the fort. They then reformed, and, restorming, carried the ditch and the outside of the work, the supports having fallen a short distance to the rear in slight disorder.[23]

Combined with a hailstorm of canister from Robinett, the Ohio units opened upon the advancing Rebels. Meanwhile, W.H.H. Minturn saw, "His leading Color Sergeant falls, when Rogers, picking up the colors, continues to advance with flag in hand."[24]

As the second surge pressed forward, some of the Rebels managed to reach the ditch in front of Robinett. Labuzan continued:

I rushed to the ditch of the Fort right between some large cannon. I grappled into it and half way up the sloping walls. The enemy were only 3 or 4 feet from me on the other side but could not shoot us for fear of having their own heads blown off. Our men were in the same predicament. Only 5 or 6 were in the wall and 30 or 40 in and around the ditch. Oh we were butchered like dogs as we were not supported. Some one placed a white handkerchief on Sergeant Buck's musket and he took it to a port hole but the Yankees snatched it off and took him prisoner the men were falling ten at a time. Our boys were shot down again like hogs and could not stand it and fell back each man for himself.[25]

The Rebels retired twenty to thirty yards and reformed and Battery Williams ceased its fire for fear of hitting Union troops. Confederate Lieutenant Labuzan of the 42nd Alabama continues his tale:

What a sight was there I saw men running at full speed stop suddenly and fall on their faces with their brains scattered all around with legs or arms cut off shrieking within a few feet of me. I gave myself to God and got ahead of my company....I seemed to be marching right in the mouth of cannon for the air was filled with bursting grape and canister while ahead was one continued blaze....As our men retreated the enemy poured on them fire and I was hardly 30 feet from the mouth of their cannon minie balls filled the stump I was behind and the shells burst within 3 or 4 feet of me. One was so close that it stunned me and burnt my face with powder the grape shot knocked large pieces of my stump off

41

*gradually wearing it away I endured the horrors of death here a
half hour and endeavored to resign myself and prayed.*[26]

Captain Jackson recalled the moment:

*...we would not fight those men any more today, as I thought it
would be impossible to rally them again, but strange to say, in some
forty minutes I saw them reformed and coming at us again with
that slow, steady step, but they made a change in their tactics, for
as they came over the bank, or rather out of the ravine in front so
us, they came at us with a yell on the double-quick.... They dashed
themselves against us like water against a rock and were a second
time repulsed and gave back.*[27]

The 2nd Texas banner fell for a fourth time and again the
Colonel seized it, riding back to rally his men reforming them for
another try at Henry Robinett and his battery all while under intense
fire from the redoubt. As Rogers rode among his men and urged
them forward for another attempt, Rebel sharpshooters crawled
forward to take out Yankee officers. With a yell, the third charge
began from about forty yards away. As numerous Confederates
huddled in the ditch below the guns, Robinett ordered his men
to hurl hand grenades[28] over the ramparts into the mass of below.
McKinstry again recalled:

*Only a remnant now of those who started, pressed on and reached
the outside of the fort, and for a moment had protection; but
before we could scarcely catch a breath, hand-grenades came flying
thick and fast over the walls of the fort, and, falling in the dust,
which was ankle deep, began to explode under our feet, filling the
air with dust and smoke, and wounding our men. It took but a
moment, however; to put a stop to this; for, having been educated
in the tactics of fort defense, we quickly answered the command
of a comrade, "Pick them up, boys, and pitch them back into the
fort;" and immediately these infernal machines were bursting upon
the inside among those who first threw them.*[29]

Captain David Jackson later recalled:

The rebel officer in command of the Texans was marching at the left of his men and when he came nigh us he turned and walked backwards and said to his men, "Boys, when you charge, give a good yell." I heard his command distinctly and it almost made the hair stand up on my head. The next instant the Texans began yelling like savages and rushed us without firing.[30]

W.H.H. Minturn of the 63rd Ohio caught a glimpse of Colonel Rogers through the smoke and confusion:

I shall ever remember looking at the face of the rebel Col. Rogers, when not more than 30 paces, and noting the peculiar expression it had. He looked neither to the right or left, neither at his own or our men, but with eyes partly closed, like one in a hail storm was marching slowly and steadily upon us.[31]

With the battery seriously in danger of being overrun, Colonel Sprague of the 63rd Ohio ordered Captain Jackson to move his company forward to Robinett.

Colonel Rogers pressed the attack and reached Battery Robinett, firing his pistol into the fortification as a few dozen of his men entered the position. Hand to hand fighting ensued. "One eyewitness stated that 'it seemed as though hell was holding a jubilee.' It was a bloody contest and we could see men using their bayonets like pitch forks and thrusting each other through."[32] The fighting was as intense and impassioned as any in the entire war. McKinstry remarked,

Some one at this juncture shouted, "Over the walls, and drive them out;" and up the steep embankment we clambered. Comrade Luke was on my right, and Comrade Franks was on my left. As we scaled the top of the parapet, a volley of musketry met us. Luke went on over, Franks was killed with a bullet in the forehead, and, as he fell backward, he clinched me around the neck and carried me tumbling back with him to the bottom of the ditch on the outside.[33]

It was then that Captain Jackson's men executed one of the more unusual occurrences of the war.

I saw that he would strike us before we could get another volley at them and I gave the command, "Don't load, boys; they are too close on you; let them have the bayonet. In a second every bayonet was brought down to a charge. I have never lived through moments of such intense excitement. Events happened quicker that I can record them. The rebels rushed toward us and just before they struck, I yelled, "Charge!" in order to give my men momentum to meet the shock. My men sprang at the enemy as one man. It reminded me of a man cutting heavy grain, striking at a thick place. The hostile guns clashed. For an instant, we parried like boxers, when the enemy gave back, firing at us now for the first as they retired.[34]

The psychological impact of the bayonet was, in most cases, far more powerful than its actual use. Bayonet charges where the enemy stood his ground were rare in the war, and a counter-charge with bayonets leading to a bayonet *fight* even more so. The only condition under which a bayonet fight can occur is when both sides choose to stand and exchange blows in close quarters. This was one of those rare times. That Robinett's redoubt positioned on the flank of the 63rd Ohio undoubtedly encouraged the men to hold their ground, for a withdrawal would place them in open ground behind the battery making them even more vulnerable.[35]

Inside Battery Robinett was a bedlam of hand-to-hand fighting, smoke, and shot. As members of the battery were falling all around him, a Minnie ball struck Robinett, laying back his scalp and knocking him unconscious and he fell under one of the guns. Seeing Robinett collapse, his men retreated from the position to take up their muskets a few yards to the rear. The position devolved into mass confusion and disorder as Rogers tried to rally his men without support to complete the assault. E. L. Lybarger of the 43rd Ohio wrote in the *National Tribune*:

The fighting in front of Robinett was desperate in the extreme. Many of the gunners from the 1st Inf. were disabled, and when the cannon ceased to belch forth its hail it was soldiers from Capt. Spangler's Co. A. 43rd Ohio, who sprang into the fort and assisted in manning the guns until the close of the struggle.[36]

This is most likely out of sequence because, as Captain Williams, in his report, noted:

The men of the First U.S. Infantry, after having been driven from their guns (they manned the siege guns), resorted to their muskets, and were firing from the musket of the embrasures at the enemy on the outside, a distance of about 10 feet intervening; but the rebels, having gained the top of the work, our men fell back into the angle of the fort, as they had been directed to do in such an emergency. Two shells were thrown from Battery Williams into Battery Robinett, one bursting on top of it and the other near the right edge. In the mean while the Eleventh Missouri Volunteers (in reserve) changed front, and, aided by the Forty-third and Sixty-third Ohio Volunteers, with the Twenty-seventh Ohio Volunteers on their right, gallantly stormed up to the right and left of the battery, driving the enemy before them. The battery could not open on the retreating enemy, for its commander, Lieutenant Robinett was wounded, and 13 of the 26 men that manned it were either killed or wounded.[37]

Those two shells would have decimated the 43rd Ohio if they were in the redoubt at that time.

W.H.H. Minturn of the 63rd Ohio supports the account of Captain Williams when he described the action:

Looking northwest along the Memphis & Charleston, RR Battery Williams, the Covered Way and Battery Robinett after the battle. Courtesy of Corinth Interpretative Center

At this most of his men ran to the rear. The firing stops as rebels gain the redoubt-13 Rebels stand upon the parapets of redoubt talking to COL Rogers when the 63rd & 42nd Ohio & 11 MO counter attack. A moment later, some of the men of Co. A. of the 43rd Ohio, entered the battery, aided the few brave fellows who had stood their ground, to man the guns.[38]

Was Robinett's wound serious? Numerous accounts mention his wounding, yet Robinett never mentioned the nature of the wound in his letters. It was only after the war, in 1867, when he applied for a disability pension and solicited a sworn statement from the surgeon who attended him at Corinth that more detailed information came to light. In a letter written on May 27, 1867, the surgeon confirmed the seriousness of the wound:

This is to certify that I attended Lieut. (Now Bvt. Maj.) H. C. Robinett, 1st U.S. Infy. Who was wounded on or about the 4th day of October, 1862 at the battle of Corinth, Miss. He was wounded by a musket ball transing the entire length of the top of his head from before, backwards, completely exposing the bone, No evidence of fracture, could be discerned. He was under my care at Corinth, Miss until sent North. J.L.G. Happensett CPT, Asst. Surgeon[39]

From this point forward, events occurred both within and outside Robinett's control that stemmed from this day and this wound. This proved to be the defining moment of his life and had a profound impact upon his military career. It is quite likely Henry suffered a concussion, today referred to as Mild Traumatic Brain Injury (MTBI).[40] This handful of hours on a hot October Thursday morning, in northern Mississippi, would irrevocably alter Robinett's life.

While Robinett was down, the Unionist 11th Missouri, positioned behind Battery Robinett, wheeled, moved forward, and engaged the Texans in front of the battery. This proved to be the undoing of the Rebel assault. Colonel Rogers, still mounted, reached for a ramrod, and tied his handkerchief around it signaling for the Yankees to hold fire. In the adrenalin rush of the moment, the signal was either not seen, ignored, or came too late and Rogers was struck at least seven times. Both rider and horse collapsed.[41] McKinstry recounted:

I heard the shout of "Victory! Victory!" and I thought we had won the day. I ran to the left of the fort whence the shout of victory came, and joined a small squad of our men that were standing a few paces from the fort. Col. Rogers and Capt. Foster were in this squad.... 'Twas then that Capt. Foster shouted, "Cease firing, men! cease firing!" and waved his handkerchief, and I realized the true situation. 'Twas too late! That fatal volley had been turned on our little band from the muzzles of fifteen hundred muskets. I looked, and, lo! every one of the fifteen men who were standing with me had fallen in a heap. I looked again, and not a Confederate was in sight. The battle was lost, and our men had fallen back to the cover of the woods. So far as I know, I am the only person near Col. Rogers when he fell who was not killed with him.[42]

Captain E.L. Lybarger, 43rd Ohio Volunteers heaped adulation upon Rogers:

I have always regretted that so intrepid a soldier, tho a dangerous enemy, was doomed to die; and I doubt very much, indeed if ever greater bravery or daring was displayed upon the field of battle by any Field Marshal of France under the eye of the great Napoleon than was exhibited by Col. Rogers in the assault on Robinett earned for him the proud distinction of 'the bravest' of the 'brave' and who led the 'Old Guard' in its last charge at Waterloo. No human courage could long withstand such fearful carnage as our guns were making, and again the enemy was compelled to fallback, this time in utter rout and disorder.[43]

The assault on Battery Robinett was over and it was just noon. As the Rebel forces fell back, Captain Minturn noted another untimely incident that added a poignant stain to the day's blood and gore.

The enemy was now retreating and in the excitement a little drummer boy passed directly before the battery and jumped upon a log to see the rebels run. A piece had just been aimed, and 'ready-fire' followed before the little fellow was discovered. When the smoke cleared up we saw that both his legs were torn off. Somehow there seemed a sting in the recollection that men of his own regiment had fired this shot.[44]

His observation here is highly romanticized and was not noted by anyone else on the field.

Almost immediately after the wounding of the young boy, Minturn witnessed a Rebel soldier who gained the admiration of the victorious Union troops:

But there was one red flag, I think the banner briefly borne by Col. Rogers, which escaped us as by a miracle. Some bold Texan had picked it up almost beneath our feet, and throwing the staff across his shoulder ran a zig-zag manner for the woods. He dodges behind a log a moment here, then behind a stump there. He was fired at by 20 men or more, and once, whether hit or not, tumbled headlong while striding a fallen tree. Yet he escaped with the banner after all, and as he passed over the ridge out of our sight, some of our boys who had missed him gave him three cheers that was due a hero.[45]

He must have mistaken an inverted Texas flag for a red one.

By noon Confederate forces were withdrawing from Corinth and the battle was over. Samuel Byers immediately went to the aid of the wounded and dying Rebel soldiers.

When the assault had failed and the noise of the battle was stilled, I hurried down in front of Robinett. My canteen was full of water and I pressed it to the lips of many a dying enemy--enemy no longer. Our grape shot had torn whole companies of men to pieces. They lay in heaps of dozens, even close up to the works.[46]

In front of Battery Robinett after the battle. Courtesy of Corinth Interpretative Center

Body of Col. Rogers after the battle (with beard) – Battery Robinett is out of the photo
to the right - courtesy of Corinth Interpretive Center

General Rosecrans did not witness the Rebel assault upon Robinett but, after hearing of his exploits, commented on the actions of Colonel Rogers. According to the Handbook of Texas:

> *In a remarkable tribute to Rogers's personal bravery, General Rosecrans ordered his burial attended with full military honors, a ceremony normally reserved only for Confederate general officers. In 1912 the United Daughters of the Confederacy, together with several Rogers family descendants, dedicated a white marble obelisk to mark his gravesite atop a hill overlooking the battlefield.*[47]

Confederate General Van Dorn also commented on Colonel Rogers and the 2nd Texas:

> *I cannot refrain, however, from mentioning here the conspicuous gallantry of a noble Texas, whose deeds at Corinth are the constant*

theme of both friends and foes. As long as courage, manliness, fortitude, patriotism, and honor exits the name of Rogers will be revered and honored among men. He fell in the front of battle, and died beneath the colors of his regiment, in the very center of the enemy's stronghold. he sleeps, and glory is his sentinel.[48]

That night Samuel Byers remembered:

That night I stood guard under an oak tree. On the battlefield under the unburied dead. Many of the wounded, even, had not yet been gathered up. The moon shone as brightly as the night before, while thousands who had laid there under its peaceful rays before the battle were now again sleeping, never to awaken again. This would not be the last encounter between Henry Robinett and the Texans.[49]

Corinth was a turning point in the western theater. General Sherman called the battle a decisive blow to the Confederate cause that forced the Confederacy to lose the strategic initiative.[50] After Corinth, the Union's way was clear to Vicksburg and Rebel General Braxton Bragg ended his Kentucky invasion in part due to a fear for his flank. It is also quite possible that if the Union forces had not prevailed, Grant would have been forced to return to the "store clerk obscurity he enjoyed prior to the war."[51] Battery Robinett's role in this critical engagement cannot be overstated. The staunch defense by Lieutenant Robinett and the men of the 1st U.S. Infantry, played a decisive part in thwarting the Rebel advance.

The Aftermath of Battle

In the coming days, Lieutenant Robinett had his wound tended and on October 28, was granted leave to return to Wilmington to complete his recovery with his family and to receive accolades as a war hero, with a promotion to brevet captain for his "gallant, determined defense of Battery Robinett" at Corinth on that fateful day in October, 1862.[52]

In Wilmington, Henry found the wartime border city bustling with Union work in everything from the construction of ironclads and steam gunboats to the manufacture of woolen cloth and military ambulances. Immigrants from the British Isles, both Irish and English, streamed in to feed these industries. [53] Regiments of volunteers mustered in to service through the summer, while secessionists still attempted to foment disorder and Fort Delaware became a prisoner-of-war camp. Concerned about the upcoming election, and fearful of an anti-war coalition, the Republican party of Delaware requested that Federal troops supervise the ballot. After a low and bitter campaign, the Democrats accused the Republicans of attempting to steal the election yet the Democrats captured control of the State and House.[54] All this bickering must have amused a man that, home from war, had seen so much in his young life.

Henry was sufficiently recovered by November 18th to petition the Lafayette Lodge #14 of the Delaware Freemasons for membership.[55] He was crafted and raised in the Lodge ten days later. This was one more piece in his ambitious drive to build a successful professional military career. There were many Freemason civil and military leaders, as well as common soldiers during the period, and thousands of recorded occasions in which one Mason assisted another on the opposite side. In future years, Robinett would call upon his lodge brothers for assistance and, in one case, no one would answer.[56]

As the new year dawned, Robinett busied himself catching up with family affairs and exploring other potential avenues for his advancement. Meanwhile, the 1st U.S. Infantry, as part of Grant's Army of the West prepared for the Vicksburg campaign, and moved from Corinth to Memphis; Major Maurice Maloney in command. Meanwhile on January 7, 1863, Robinett, was afforded another honor; a select group of Wilmington citizens presented him with a ceremonial saber inscribed: "Corinth/Sept 3rd & 4th/1862/Presented to Lieut. Henry Clay Robinett by citizens of Wilmington, Del. As a tribute to worth and valor," and accompanied by a note reading:

A number of your fellow citizens of Wilmington appreciating your courage and skill displayed at the Battle of Corinth, Miss. Nov [Oct] 3 & 4 1862 beg that you will accept the accompanying SWORD, SASH and BELT as a testimonial of their regard. Very truly your friends. Edward W. Gilpin, Evan C. Stotsenburg, Daniel James, Theo. Rogers" [57]

Previously, Henry had joined the "right" church and the "right" fraternal organization. Once again, Henry had made the right connections with the rich and powerful in Wilmington through his membership at Holy Trinity Church. Theodore B. Rogers was also a member of the church. The Gilpin Family was and is a prominent Delaware family and many were members of Henry's church, though Edward was not. Stotsenburg was a foundry owner and sat on the boards of The Artisans Bank, Bank of Delaware, Bank of Wilmington & Brandywine, and Delaware Fire Company. He was a member of the 4th Delaware Volunteers in 1862 and later a member of the Knights of Pythias. [58] Daniel James was one of the original directors of the First National Bank of Wilmington in 1864, Vice President of the Union League of Wilmington 1863. Daniel does not appear in the church records, but there are others from his family listed. Edward W. Gilpin became the fifth chief justice under the Constitution of Delaware in 1831 and served as Attorney General for the state for ten years. For many years, he was president of the Union National Bank and a director of the Philadelphia, Wilmington and Baltimore, and Delaware Railroad. [59] These men all resided or had business addresses within a several block radius and were close friends. Henry definitely knew who could help his career and these ties would pay off for him in the coming years.

Robinett's ceremonial saber - courtesy Delaware Historical Society

Endnotes

1. OR, Series I—Volume XVII/ [S# 24] p. 247.

2. Chance, 66.

3. Cornelison, John E Jr, Tammy D. Cooper. "Archeological Investigations of Battery Robinett and the Confederate Attack on Corinth." Shiloh National Military Park, 2004.

4. Byers, Samuel H.M. Major. "With Fire and Sword." New York: Neale Publishing Company, 1911, p. 33-34.

5. Minturn. W.H.H. "Battle of Corinth, Fuller's Ohio Brigade and the Part it Took in This Engagement. National Tribune, May 23, 1901.

6. The note is found on Roger's body, vest pierced by bullets, a portion of which is on display on museum of Wisconsin Historical Society, Madison, WI (Chance)

7. Cockrell, Monroe F. "The Lost Account of the Battle of Corinth and the Court Martial of Gen. Van Dorn." Jackson, TN: Mercer Press, 1855, p. 31.

8. Stevens, Charles. "The Corinth Diary of Private Charles Stevens Company A, 47th Illinois Infantry." Danville, VA: Blue and Gray Education Society, 2006.

9. Cozzens, 234.

10. McKinstry, J.A. With Col. Rogers When He Fell. Confederate Veteran, Vol. 4, No. 7, Nashville, July 1896.

11. Stevens, 19-20.

12. Labuzan, Charles C. "1st Lt. Letter." Greenville Dodge Papers, Iowa State Historical Library.

13. Cozens, 234.

14. Ibid.

15. McKinstry.

16. Jackson, David Prentice, ed. "The colonel's diary; journals kept before and during the civil war by the late Colonel Oscar L. Jackson...sometime commander

of the 63rd regiment O. V. I." Sharon, PA: 1922. p. 71. At this point Jackson is a Captain.

17. Byers, 35-36.

19. McKinstry.

20. Cozzens, 258.

21. Jackson, 72.

22. Chance, Letter from Thomas Hagan to his father, Oct 22, '62.

23. OR, SERIES I--VOLUME XVII/1 [S# 24] p. 248.

24. Minturn. W.H.H. "Battle of Corinth, Fuller's Ohio Brigade and the Part it Took in This Engagement." National Tribune, May 23, 1901.

25. Ibid.

26. Labuzan.

27. Jackson, 73.

28. Most likely not formal hand grenades as developed during the war but rather simply explosive shells.

29. McKinstry.

30. Jackson, 74.

31. Minturn.

32. Dossman, Steven Nathaniel. "Campaign for Corinth: Blood in Mississippi." Abilene, TX: McWhiney Foundation Press, 2006, 119.

33. McKinstry.

34. Jackson, 74.

35. For an excellent discussion of bayonet tactics and their effects see Brent Nosworthy's "The Bloody Crucible of Courage: Fighting Methods and Combat Experience of the Civil War." New York: Carroll & Graf, 2003.

36. Lybarger, E. L. "The Battle of Corinth." National Tribune, November 26, 1908.

37. OR Series I--Volume XVII/1 [S# 24] p. 248.

38. Minturn.

39. Letters Received by the Commission of the Adjutant General's Office, 1861-1870; (National Archives Microfilm Publication Main Series, Roll 578); 1867, 214-279.

40. "Mild traumatic brain injury (MTBI), a physical as opposed to an emotional injury, is caused from a relatively mild blow to the brain that causes just enough physical injury that normal brain functions of memory, attention, mental organization, and logical thinking may be compromised. MTBI, as opposed to more severe brain injury, is diagnosed when the length of unconsciousness is less than 30 minutes and when there is no more than a 24-hour loss of memory for the event. Sometimes loss of consciousness can be momentary and amnesia only fragmented for a few hours. With virtually no alteration in consciousness nor amnesia, occurrence of brain injury should be highly suspect." Mild Traumatic Brain Injury vs. Post-Traumatic Stress Disorder Dennis P. Swiercinsky, Ph.D. http://www.brainsource.com/mtbivs.htm accessed 25 August 2009. See also Report to Congress on Mild Traumatic Brain Injury in the United States: Steps to Prevent a Serious Public Health Problem. National Center for Injury Prevention and Control, Centers for Disease Control and Prevention. http://www.cdc.gov/ncipc/pub-res/mtbi/mtbireport.pdf accessed 25 August 2009. "The conceptual definition of MTBI is an injury to the head as a result of blunt trauma or acceleration or deceleration forces that result in one or more of the following conditions: Any period of observed or self-reported: Transient confusion, disorientation, or impaired consciousness; Dysfunction of memory around the time of injury; Loss of consciousness lasting less than 30 minutes. Symptoms among older children and adults such as headache, dizziness, irritability, fatigue, or poor concentration, when identified soon after injury, can be used to support the diagnosis of mild TBI."

41. Cozzens, 265.

42. McKinstry.

43. Lybarger.

44. Minturn.

45. Ibid.

46. Byers, 36.

47. Handbook of Texas Online.

48. OR SERIES I--VOLUME XVII/1 [S# 24] p. 381. In another tribute: "Col. Rogers left to his children the legacy of an unsullied name, and a fame that will live while a Southern heart throbs with love for, and pride in, this sunny Southland of ours" found in Cockrell, Monroe F. "The Lost Account of the Battle of Corinth and the Court Martial of Gen. Van Dorn." Jackson, TN: Mercer Press, 1855. After being captured on October 4th, 1st Lieutenant Charles Labuzan wrote, "Right at our charging place the dead men were piled in heaps Gatsby not there. I saw Col. Rogers stripped he was shot with four balls and Capt. Foster his brains all on the ground. The stump I was behind is literally cut to pieces by cannon shot and to within a few inches of my head. Some had flesh shot off their bones and other limbs in little pieces. Those killed were mostly from grapeshot the fire here was so terrible that hardly a man had less than two bullets in him and in many I counted five or six."

49. Byers, 35-36.

50. Dossman, 135.

51. Cozzens, xi.

52. Letters Received by the Commission of the Adjutant General's Office, 1861-1870; (National Archives Microfilm Publication Main Series, Roll 578); 1867, 214-279.

53. Reed, 20.

54. Ibid. 25.

55. While this is a very rapid progression, it was and still is not unusual for a lodge to suspend normal procedures for a man temporarily home from war. In another occurrence Daniel Citron, a member of the Lodge and Historic Site Manager, Auburn Heights Preserve wrote me, "I have seen this before with a soldier in Jackson Lodge. The first commander of Fort Delaware, Captain A. A. Gibson, petitioned to join the lodge. Two months later, he received all three degrees on the same night. The lodge had received a special dispensation to do this. Looking at the timing of it, it was because Capt. Gibson knew he was going to be transferred to Washington D.C. and wanted to become a mason in Jackson

Lodge because he was so moved by their Masonic funeral service for the first Confederate POW that died at Fort Delaware." I am deeply indebted to Robert Benson, Worshipful Master of the Lafayette Lodge, as well as his brothers in the lodge for his assistance with this project.

56. This is known as an "on site mason" and was quite common for soldiers on leave.

57. The saber, complete with scabbard and case, was recently donated to the Delaware Historical Society by Mr. and Mrs. NormanCol Taylor. I talked to them to discover the circumstances of the donation and to ask how the saber remained in such pristine condition. Jeanne Taylor's aunt, Doris Robinette Favinger passed at the age of 92. As executors of the estate, they went through her house and found IN THE ATTIC, on the floor, papers belonging to Henry C. Robinett as well as the saber. The materials descended in the family to Joseph Allen Williams (1880-1939) Henry's great nephew. The papers included all of Robinett's commissioning documents, post cards with engravings of the battle of Corinth, genealogy pages from a family Bible, and a photo of Henry. I am deeply indebted to the folks at the Historical Society, especially, Constance J. Cooper, Director of Library at DHS for all her assistance in the past two years.

58. The Order of Knights of Pythias is an international, non-sectarian fraternal order, established in 1864 in Washington, DC, by Justus H. Rathbone. At President Lincoln's suggestion, nn application was made to Congress for a charter, and the Order of Knights of Pythias became the first American Order ever chartered by an Act of the Congress of the United States. The distinguishing principles of the Order of Knights of Pythias are "FRIENDSHIP, CHARITY and BENEVOLENCE." It bases its lessons and builds it ritual largely on the familiar story of the friendship of Damon and Pythias, who were historical characters living about four hundred or more years before the beginning of the Christian era. http://www.pythias.org/index.html

59. Scharff, J. Thomas. "History of Delaware 1609-1888." (Philadelphia: L.J. Richards & Co. 1888), p. 534-4 & Holy Trinity Church Records, Wilmington 1800-1860.

Chapter IV:
"Metallic Friends"

Return to War

By the end of January of 1863, Henry was preparing to rejoin his regiment. In February, he arrived in time to participate in the reduction of Fort Pemberton on March 11th during the Yazoo Pass Expedition.[1]   By this time, the 1st U.S. Infantry was attached to the 14th Division commanded by Brigadier General Eugene Asa Carr, under Major General J. A. McClernand's Thirteenth Corps.

According to *The Army of the United States, Historical Sketches of Staff and Line with Portraits of Generals-in-Chief*, "On the 22nd of March, General McClernand was directed to forward at once to the Yazoo Pass an expedition of four 30 pound Parrotts, with not less than 80 men of the 1st Infantry, to be under the command of Captain G. A. Williams, but as General Grant wrote on the same day that, 'It is now clearly demonstrated that a further force, in by way of Yazoo Pass, can be of no service,' it is probable that this order did not go into effect."[2]   Henry refuted this in a letter to his brother Theodore on April 12th from Milliken's Bend, Henry describes this expedition in great detail:

I had been away on an expedition sent to reduce Fort Pemberton, near Greenwood, Miss. Parts of the companies of our Battalion mine among the list were ordered there after the failure of the attempt to capture it by the Gunboats in conjunction with the army, consisting of about five thousand men at first, afterwards increased to eight thousand. We had quite a tedious, irksome and difficult trip, so far as navigation was concerned. I think in all your seamanship experience you never experienced such almost insurmountable difficulty as we encountered. I am confident it would have been perplexing and supremely disgusting to you even, who have likely been subjected to the caprices and hardships of the "briny deep." No jesting about it, I'll assure you. We entered the [Yazoo] Pass from the Miss. river near Helena Aks(sic) (10 miles below), and the current was so rapid we were carried through it to Moon Lake, a distance of two miles, like a ship driven before the wind by the fiercest gale of the stormy Atlantic; On Friday 27th of March. We did not reach the end of the Pass until four days later. Our run in the Lake – three miles was plain sailing, but our passage through the lower portion of the Pass – 14 miles was horribly slow. One day we accomplished the remarkably great distance of one mile. The cannel(sic) of the water course was nearly sixty feet in width; then of the steamer fifty, and her length one hundred and eighty. It was more zig zag and serpentine than could possibly imagine; you would have to see it to have a fair idea of its crookedness. Old "Meander" himself could never have been half as winding in course. The helm of the boat was a vanity in such a body of water, and had to be actually abandoned: the chief dependence was put in the favorable jutting trees along each side of the channel: they alternately (sic) at stem and stern, by running against them, veering her and giving her the proper direction. The "Pass" is a channel made through an enormous swamp – such as you find in this Southern country – by clearing it of trees, and other impediments to navigation that exist in such places. Don't you fancy you would have enjoyed such a trip? We saw nothing for three days but a wilderness of woods and water. Not a habitation of a civilized being gladdened our eyes. After "getting out of the wilderness," (the Pass) we had a hundred and eight miles farther. Although the greatest part of our march was over a prairie which was under ten inches of water and covered with high grass, and the road was very heavy and nearly knee deep before we would arrive at our destination. After leaving the Pass the rest of our journey was on the Coldwater and Tallahatchie rivers. Neither of them was a great impediment in width or more favorable to navigation. Than the Pass, especially for our large boat. We had to abandon our boat and transfer to another smaller size when within a hundred miles of Fort Pemberton, on the Tallahatchie. We had disabled the wheel -- the boat Dacotah (sic) is a "stern wheeler" – several times, but in striking with it against the shore it was shattered almost to pieces, so much so as to be perfectly useless. The boat was indeed a sad spectacle. Guards, nearly all of the Hurricane deck, smoke stacks and stern pipes carried away and broken; jack staff dismantled, kitchen torn away and emptied into the river, as well as the store room, left her quite bereft of her former symmetry and beauty of entireness. A slight incident to a soldier's life occurred just as we issued from the lower end of the Pass into the Coldwater—it proved its name a liberty as the sequel will show. A party of Guerrillas fired into our boat; their fire was directed principally upon a group of officers, I being one of the number, and the Pilot. I suppose they fired in all about twenty shots, only one of which took effect seriously. One man of my company, which was standing between the fire and the officers, and no doubt received the ball intended for one of us, was struck, the ball passed through his right fore arm and lodged in his hip: another, a corporal, (same company) had his neck handkerchief and the button of his shirt collar shot off by a bullet. These cowardly villains, fit only for such warfare scampered before we could return fire. They were concealed in the canebreak at the water's edge.

After reaching our destination to our chagrin and great disappointment we were informed the expedition or rather the object of it was about being abandoned. And we of course did not have an opportunity to "fire a single gun" at misguided defenders of rebeldom. Two days after our arrival we were on the "right about" to Millikens Bend after leaving the rebels to chuckle over our failure to take their strong hold. I imagine another tale would have been told had the 1st Infty. been permitted to open fire upon their works with our "Pet Parrotts." We were all, of course, greatly displeased with the result. It is the first "retrograde movement" we have ever had the ill fortune to participate in.[3]

This adventure, as told by Robinett, was quite an ordeal and considering the sloughs and bayous of the area, would appear to be an accurate description of travel through "The Pass."

Henry was obviously looking to make a name for himself and his "Pet Parrotts" and, in this case, was fairly disappointed by the lack of opportunity. Now full of *braggadocio,* he continued and speculated about future operations against Vicksburg.

Nothing's very interesting has occurred since my arrival here, which was two days ago. If movement was on foot, which it is to cross the river from the Louisiana shore below Vicksburg, if it is successful, and there is nothing at present to prevent it, Vicksburg must soon "be ours." I really suppose before this reaches you, news to that effect will flash across the wires to your "Pacific shores."

We have a very pleasant encampment at present; all that could be desired, plenty of shade (we have need for it here even in March and April) and other conveniences. I have seen a little hardship since I left home from "Sick Leave" But as that you know being soldiers, we do not take much offense or complain loudly, as it is all to be expected, in such a part of our "discipline." [4]

The end of April and the beginning of May found the 1st U.S. Infantry on the move as part of Grant's Vicksburg Campaign. On the 16th they participated in the battle of Champions Hill, behind the center of the Union line, supporting Lindsey's Brigade and shelling Rebel breastworks.

The 2nd Texas and on to Vicksburg

Meanwhile, the 2nd Texas moved into fortifications commanding the Baldwin Ferry Road, a key position in the southern sector of the line surrounding Vicksburg. The 2nd Texas lunette was half moon shaped, on a hill with two embrasures[5] for cannon with a traverse[6] between. The parapet was four and a half feet tall on the inside with a slope fourteen feet thick and protected by a six-foot deep ditch. Somewhat forward of the Rebel line, the position could only hold four companies; the two others were in rifle pits on the right flank of the position. Four more companies were on the left flank separated by 100-yards of open space through which Baldwin Ferry Road ran. The area facing the position was hilly on both sides, enabling plunging fire into the lunette.[7] Immediately the 2nd Texas began improving the position to create clear lines of fire. They burned several houses in front of the position and chopped down numerous trees. They also increased the parapet to six feet so riflemen could fire from within. They dug rifle pits behind fortifications, and each soldier was issued five or six additional muskets loaded with buck and ball.[8]

The 1st U.S. Infantry approached Vicksburg after the battle of Champion Hill, moving their siege guns into position. On the 19th of May, at 10 A.M. McClernand's artillery opened; Robinett in a reversal of Corinth began to shell the 2nd Texas fortifications. He was in command of the guns supporting the 14th Division consisting of four 30-pound Parrotts.[9] One soldier from the 2nd Texas remembered the barrage:

Some idea may be formed of the artillery fire to which we were exposed, when I state that a small party went out for that purpose collected some two thousand shells near and in the rear of the trenches occupied by our brigade.[10]

At 2 P.M. the McClernand's infantry stepped off as Rebel artillery opened. The attack stalled and McClernand eventually cancelled the assault. During the night, Robinett worked (at extreme personal risk) to move a gun closer to the Texans to provide close support for the infantry in its next assault. On the 21st, Robinett's battery fired with deadly effectiveness and disabled two guns in the lunette while heavily damaging the earthworks.

At daybreak on May 22nd McClernand's opened with all twenty-two guns in the area, knocking holes in earthworks. The Rebel guns fell silent. One Rebel counted up to forty shells a minute striking the position in "one continuous roar."[11] The Union attack stepped off but stalled around 11 A.M., and a second attempt in the afternoon also failed. The siege of Vicksburg had begun.

During the ensuing siege, Robinett would continue to lob 30-pound Parrott shells on Rebel positions. "The regiment added greatly to its reputation for gallantry and efficient service during the siege and, though always on duty at the front, met with little loss."[12] Later, because of his service at Vicksburg, Brigadier General Eugene A. Carr recommended him for "two or more brevets." In a letter to Major General Rawlins, Chief of Staff to General Grant, he wrote:

> *I mentioned him favorably in my official report...but it seems that the report never came before the commanding general...it must have worked a great injustice to the Officers and Soldiers of my Division as well as myself. Lieut Robinett showed great gallantry and skill during the whole time he was with me - particularly in taking up an advanced position during the night of May 19th and silencing the enemies batteries next morning, in exploding rebel magazines, in covering and supporting our troops during the assault of the 22 May and in being exposed to the fire of sharpshooters during the whole siege.[13]*

To the Paris of America

When the siege ended on July 4, 1864, the 1st U.S. was ordered to New Orleans, to be stationed in the city and quartered in Odd Fellows' Hall opposite Lafayette Park where the unit became the provost guard. Henry wrote his brother Theodore on December 2, to catch him up on his escapades:

> *Our regiment did not go to Natchez as Pap wrote you. We left Vicksburg on the 24th of Aug. and arrived at Carrollton, La which is five miles from N.O. Aug 27th, where we remained until Oct 5th when we started for the Teche [Bayou] country. We had our Siege guns turned over at Carrollton before leaving for that campaign. I grieved a good deal at their loss, for we had achieved*

such splendid results with them and had them so long that we formed quite an attachment for "our Pet Parrotts". They were needed for the fortifications so we yielded to the "military necessity" with as good grace as possible. Notwithstanding the necessity we could not stifle our regrets and feel that we had been harshly and probably unfairly dealt with in being separated from such tired and true "Metallic Friends." [14]

Robinett was not looking forward to life as an infantry officer. He enjoyed his "pet Parrots" and the renown they brought him. In addition, there may not have been enough glory in the Department of the Gulf for him. "I do not like the Department as well as others I have served in. I would much prefer being in Gen. Grant's Command. We were all quite disappointed when we were transferred to this. We imagined as we had served so long under his command we would always campaign in it." He was susceptible to the rumor mill as well, "He [Grant] himself was heard to say our transfer was only temporary, otherwise he would not have permitted us to go from his Department. We have no hope at present of getting back there." This was not to be. Henry was looking for the fast track to promotions and wanted to hitch his wagon to the Grant star. Reminiscing about experiences at Corinth and Vicksburg, he tells his brother:

I am of your opinion as regards of my services at Corinth and Vicksburg. I think the Department of Washington will one day notice them, though it may be distant. You must return my sincere thanks to my friends in Sanfransico (sic) for their appreciation of the services I have rendered our glorious Republic and dear native land, and also for their excellent opinions concerning ability etc of myself their humble servant. [15]

As for New Orleans itself, Henry was quite pleased with the largest city of the South and found a schoolmate from DMA there:

We have been here a few days more than a month. I am tolerably well pleased with the city, better now than a short time after our arrival for I have found an old friend and schoolmate, C. R. May, (Will Irelan is acquainted with him) who is in a very large business here. He and I are quite intimate. I have dined with him several times of late. It makes it much more pleasant in a large city like this where a great many are enemies, as it were - Secesh - to find at least one old and tried friend with whom to associate and while away leisure hours. New Orleans is the gayest place I ever visited. I imagine it far surpassed Sanfrancisco(sic). It is surely the Paris of America. It is a continuous whirl of pleasure here with all classes of society, and it is truly astonishing how it is kept up for it is fearfully expensive. One can live fast and princely here but it tells fearfully on his finances. I have seen other places I prefer to it on that account. It is certainly one of the prettiest cities of the Union. It has a number of Public Buildings of massive and magnificent structure. Fine Squares and beautiful Statues.[16]

His observations concerning the "Secesh" citizenry was prophetic; in the coming years, New Orleans will not be so friendly to Henry Robinett.

Endnotes

1. Letters Received by the Commission of the Adjutant General's Office, 1861-1870; (National Archives Microfilm Publication Main Series, Roll 578); 1867, 214-279.

2. Rodenbough, 410.

3. "Theodore Julius Robinett (1837 -ca. 1908) was a San Francisco ship's cook and nurse who made many extended voyages. In 1860, he sailed from Philadelphia to San Francisco and from there to Hong Kong." Register of the Robinette Family Papers, 1845-1910, Robinette Family Papers, Mss183, Holt-Atherton Department of Special Collections, University of the Pacific Library. [hereafter referred to as Family Papers]

4. Family Papers, April 12, 1863 letter to Theodore Robinett.

5. An embrasure is a shaped opening in a parapet or casemate wall that allows artillery to fire through the parapet or wall. Embrasures were generally employed when it was necessary to cover artillerists serving a piece from enemy musket or artillery fire and when a piece did not require a wide field of fire. Embrasures in field fortifications were usually given a trapezoidal shape with a narrow neck through the interior slope of a parapet that gradually widened until it reached the crest of the exterior slope. Cut surfaces on either side of an embrasure were referred to as cheeks and were usually revetted (A revetment was a superficial structure designed to retain an earth slope at an angle greater than the natural angle that the soil would assume when thrown loosely into a pile.) with gabions (rough cylindrical wicker basket full of earth) or fascines (A tightly bound bundle of brushwood and small straight branches.) to stand at a slope of one unit of base to three units of altitude above the lower flat surface of the embrasure, called the sole. Dictionary of Fortifications: http://civilwarfortifications.com/dictionary/xge-001.html

6. Traverses were raised mounds of earth designed to defilade the interior spaces of field works and to limit the area effected by explosions occurring within gun positions. For the most part traverses were given a rectangular outline with the mound surfaces sloped upward and inward from the base to form a rounded peak along the upper surface or crown. Ibid., http://civilwarfortifications.com/dictionary/xgt-007.html

7. Chance, 103. Normally, a lunette consisted of four faces and three salient angles with a ditch to front and open in rear. For an interesting study of the Vicksburg campaign see: Ballard, Michael B. "Vicksburg: The Campaign That Opened the Mississippi." Chapel Hill, NC: University of North Carolina Press, 2004. One of the most detailed, intriguing examinations of Vicksburg is Warren E Grabau's "Ninety-Eight days: A Geographer's View of the Vicksburg Campaign." Knoxville, TN: The University of Tennessee Press, 2000. The maps and descriptive terrain details are superior to anything yet produced.

8. Ibid.

9. Later two 8-inch Dahlgren guns would join the battery. "Lt. Robinett was practically in charge of this battery, Maj. Maloney had supervision of all the batteries manned by the 1st U.S. Infantry." Maloney was in another area of the field commonly known at the White House near "The Crater." Regimental Files, 1st U.S. Siege Guns, Folder 532, Vicksburg National Military Park." I appreciate the assistance of Terrence Winschel, Historian at Vicksburg National Military Park in locating this information.

10. Chance, 104.

11. Ibid. 111.

12. Rodenbough, 410.

13. Records of the Office of the Judge Advocate General Court Martial Case Files, 1809-1894; (National Archives record Group 153, File OO-1898. The letter written November 23, 1865 indicated his original report did not reach General Grant nor was it included in the Os.

14. Family Papers, December 2, 1863 letter to Theodore Robinett.

15. Ibid.

16. Ibid.

Chapter V:
"I have a good position,
I must admit"

Home Again

Lieutenant Robinett, still officially unrecognized for his service at Corinth and Vicksburg, spent December and January of 1864 in New Orleans. Granted leave at this point, he returned to Wilmington where he continued to position himself for advancement. In February, Major General McClernand requested he be relieved of duty with the 1st U.S. and reassigned to his staff with the rank of brevet Captain.[1] In March, assigned to recruitment duty in Wilmington, Robinett awaited orders to report to the general's staff.[2] The assignment arrived on March 19 and Henry accepted the position two days later with the rank of Captain of Volunteers, Aide de Camp. Henry wrote in an October 4 letter to his brother Theo, "Contrary to all expectations I remained at home for more than five months. Most of the time I was on recruiting service and for a month I was awaiting orders. When I reached home from New Orleans I did not expect to stay there longer than 2 weeks at furthest." Henry contributed $100 towards his sister Lou's wedding expenses, "the pleasure of seeing her married well and happily more than repaid me." Evidently his family was not doing too well in spite of the fact that Wilmington was bustling with work, "I was of a great deal of aid to all while at home, for all were out of employment, and I furnished the edibles for my board."[3]

According to Thomas J. Reed, "The second full year (1863) fell heavily on Delaware. It was a year of terrible casualty lists from the battlefields of the Army of the Potomac, of an invasion threat to the state, of the draft and draft resistance."[4] In June, secessionist sabotage destroyed three rolling mills, a grain mill, and a loaded boxcar of gunpowder. In January of 1864, the General Assembly refused to fund Delaware's share of the soldiers' cemetery at Gettysburg and refused to vote a resolution of thanks for its soldiers. They also refused an enlistment bonus for the states' African-Americans troops yet voted an enlistment bonus for every white man who voluntarily enlisted.[5] Henry lived in a deeply conflicted and divided border state.

Captain Robinett remained on recruitment duty until July 24 when he was released from duty. Major Henry B. Judd, commander of the Military District of Wilmington, commented on his service:

Being very much in need of efficient officers to assist in mustering and organizing the volunteers, I availed myself of the presence of Paymaster F. B. Warner, U.S. Army, and Capt. H. C. Robinett, First U. S. Infantry, both of whom happened to be here on special duty….In all these labors I was indebted, for their cordial co-operation and intelligent aid.[6]

So far, everyone in the Army seemed to be pleased with his service, so on August 1st, Henry decided to take action and get his career on the move again by appealing directly to General Grant.

I have while here, detached from my regiment on recruiting Service, received a Commission of Captain & Aide-de-Camp. No orders were sent with my Commission. Subsequent to the receipt of it I was relieved from my duty on recruiting Service; but again, 'no Orders' to report to any person or place reached me. I am extremely anxious, general, to be on duty in the field! I should be delighted to serve again under the eye of 'Our Old Commander' as it was my good fortune to do in the West-particularly at Vicksburg!!! Could you not assign me to duty, general, according to my rank as Capt & A.D.C near yourself? If so I shall endeavor to justify the bestowal of the favor as I did the first you granted at Millikens Bend, LA in April 1863. I hope sincerely my request may meet with a favorable consideration, General, at your hands, for I am so weary of, and dissatisfied with my present inactivity. Please excuse the presumption (if it seem such to you) displayed in asking this favor, for my eagerness to see another siege like Vicksburg re-enacted and to be serving with you has prompted it. My Commission was forwarded to me from the War Department 2nd of April through Gen. McClerland (sic); it may be he should have sent me orders, but he did not. He is, I learned, absent from his command in a very critical state of health.[7]

While there is no evidence to prove Robinett was aware of the deep rift between McClernand and Grant, it is obvious he knew with whom to position himself.[8] Robinett saw his future in the Division of the Gulf in a less favorable light than if he were to serve with "Our Old Commander" in the east. For Robinett, after Vicksburg and the removal of his "pet Parrotts" along with his assignment to New Orleans, he felt the need to make a change. A position on McClernand's staff with the hopes of even better advancement in the future was just what he needed but he wanted more. Curiously, nowhere does he indicate what he could do to *enhance* Grant's staff. He simply states his desire to serve with Grant.

In service to General Grant

Robinett was ecstatic when he gained a minor position on Grant's staff as an assistant aide-de-camp. This was in no small part, no doubt, due to Brigadier General John A. Rawlins, Chief of Staff for General Grant and fellow Freemason. His time on the staff performing the mundane duties of a general's staff officer was mostly uneventful. Henry wrote two letters full of pride and excitement from City Point, VA to his brother Theodore, and, in typical soldier fashion, downplayed his time under fire.

I have a good position, I must admit, but although my rank is higher than when I first entered the service, really my pay is only about half what I was then on account of depreciated currency [due to inflation]. It takes a great deal to sustain ones dignity when occupying a position such as I now do….How inconvenient Theo, it is to be poor. Many a young man would give a small fortune to hold a staff appointment with Commander-in-Chief of the Armies of the United States and I may have to give it up merely because I have not the means to sustain the "dig" appertaining thereto. I shall make desperate efforts to hold on to one of the best things that our country affords at the present day. I will merely say that the military situation in this vicinity is quite cheering and we all believe that our invincible and ever victorious General will certainly go into Richmond before Christmas, maybe in a few weeks, and afterwards demolish this great rebellion in a very short time. It is my first service with the Army of the Potomac. I was out with Gen Grant on the 29 of Sept when we had such a brilliant

Gen. Ulysses S. Grant and staff of fourteen, Robinett is second from the right, to his immediate right is General Rawlings – Mathew Brady Photographs of Civil War-Era Personalities and Scenes http://narademo.umiacs.umd.edu/cgi-bin/isadg/viewitem.pl?item=40594

success near Richmond; was under fire and exposed in carrying Dispatches from the Gen to the Corps Commander. I escaped unhurt.[9]

He had a soldier's optimism as the holidays approached and in the midst of all these military matters, let a mysterious cat out of the bag to his brother, "I might get married too, in a year or two, to a fine, intelligent, interesting young lady from Wilmington. but such things cannot be without there is some cash on hand or in prospective." While at home, Henry had found a young woman suitable for his ambitions though at that point he had no intentions of saying any more.

Captain Robinett remained with Grant throughout the winter months with a short holiday break back in Wilmington. In February, he again wrote his brother still full of his youthful optimism and enthusiasm about future military operations.

I think we will not have to wait longer, at furthest, than the next Summer's campaign. For the "magnificent plans and irresistible combinations" of the greatest of all Generals (Lt. Gen. U.S. Grant) is fast using up the rebel material for an army and confusing their ablest generals and statesmen. We have other very fine subordinate generals under his command, who deserve great praise and imperishable glory for executing his plans, carrying our his orders and co-operating so harmoniously with him; but it must be thoroughly understood that he is head and shoulders above them all "in greatness and brains."[10]

Henry suffers from hero worship and a tremendous admiration for Grant. Perhaps, in his mind, Robinett hoped that one day he too could obtain such renown. He later wrote, "There are many young gentlemen of wealth that would give quite a large portion of their worldly goods for it. [Serving on Grant's staff] But it is not every one that can have the honor."[11]

Once again, with a tantalizing bit more detail, his romance emerges.

I expect to commit the great mistake of a man's life time some
time next Winter. -- "Deo volente". [God willing] What I mean is
that I expect to be married to one of the brightest most intelligent
and sweetest little women East of the Rocky Mountains next
Winter, providing I can raise the where-with-all to support such
an uncalled for luxury (--such old bachelors as yourself I suppose
would call it so). Keep the above entirely to yourself Theo let no one
home or in Cal. either know of it until I see fit to tell them. I know
you can keep a secret inviolate.[12]

Who was this mysterious woman that so enraptured Robinett?
Elsie Sherwood Starr, born on December 21, 1844. She, like
many of his other acquaintances, was a member of one of the first
families of Wilmington. Her father, Elijah Francis Starr, was a
ship captain sailing out of Wilmington. Captain Starr's wife, Anna
Crossman, came from a well-to-do family as well. Both families
were prominent members of the Holy Trinity Church. Once again,
Henry had found a way to advance his social standing and perhaps
his career ambitions.

On April 21, 1865, Robinett was promoted to Brevet
Major on the recommendation of General Grant, a position of
which he was quite proud.[13] There seemed to be only a few eventful
incidents in his career as aide-de-camp that he felt were worthy of
mentioning in his letters. He recounted one close call in a letter to
Dorie on July 15, 1865.

I rode with the General into some dangerous places – he is not at all
particular of his personal safety – and had one personal adventure.
I was carrying an order from him to General Sheridan at the time
it occurred. We had cut the rebel army in two. Gen Sheridan was
off far to the left – this left a large portion of Lee's army between
the main portion of the army of the Potomac and the army of the
James and the force Sheridan had with him. Before starting with
the order I had a rode (sic) pointed out to me as the nearest, which
I, of course, took, as time was precious and dispatch necessary. I
had not gone far before I had misgivings about the 'lay of the land'.

I had only one mounted man (Calvary man) with me. I had ridden about two miles when within sight of a house, where I had to turn abruptly to the right, I slackened my horse's gait as things began to look decidedly suspicious, -- I beckoned to a negro who was near it, he did not obey, but look (sic) suspiciously about him. Keeping on slowly, I saw a rebel infantryman step leisurly (sic) and carelessly from the house, I supposed he was going to surrender, from his careless manner, he stepped up to a tree about 150 ft from me, leveled his gun and fired at me. I thought certainly the fellow would have struck me and either wounded or killed me. The ball whistled uncomfortably near my head. I pulled my pistol as soon as he approached the tree and pointed it towards him, but did not shoot because he covered himself completely by the tree. I think this is what probably shook his nerves and he missed me. Just then 7 others made their appearance and I having to carry my orders which were very important could not engage in such an unequal combat, but rode off as fast as my good horse would carry me. The sesh fired at me while I rode away, but strange to say not a single shot took effect. I consider this one of the more fortunate escapes I have made during the war. My escape -- especially from the first fellow's fire -- was almost miraculous. I made several narrow ones during "our great and most brilliant campaign." [14]

Henry was wise to avoid such an uneven confrontation and seems quite pleased with his reaction to this encounter – another test of bravery.

An Extra Aide and Back to New Orleans

The end of the war found Robinett an "extra" aide-de-camp and as such, he was released to the 1st U.S. Infantry still on garrison duty in New Orleans. Unfortunately, there were no available slots for a Captain so Brevet Major Robinett was further reduced to 1st Lieutenant and assigned to his old unit. "I reached here on the 11th of June. I was relieved from Staff duty on the 8th of May. You will recollect I was an extra Aide-de-Camp on the Genl's Staff and as soon as the War was over he had to dispense with all his staff except those allowed by Law. I lost my rank as Capt on leaving his staff. I am still a first Lieut in my own reg't, but soon expect to be a Captain. That will be a very nice and handsome position." His ego gets the better of him as he continues, "I have very pleasant times while on the Gen's staff. He gave me a brevet Major of Vols. That does me no good now however as the war is over. If I had had political influence I could at least have been a Brig-Gen two years ago. I don't say it vainly or boastingly. I know hundreds who have had it have been made Brig and Major Genls for less distinguished services than me over in this war. I will rest content however and hope for reward in the future."[15]

Again, his thoughts turned to Elise, "I may not be able to accomplish that matter I spoke of in my last letter to you next Winter. If we are kept here I am afraid I cannot get home for the purpose." Henry Robinett's life was about to take a series of turns for the worse that would see his marriage plans dashed and his carefully planned military career in ruins.

The City of New Orleans

New Orleans after the war was a city in turmoil. Without a doubt, Louisiana had the most complex and tangled Reconstruction of any Southern state.[16] Even with the early occupation of New Orleans during the war, "not a foot of Louisiana beyond the city and outside the range of Union cannon was left in possession of the deferral forces."[17] A series of Union generals had commanded the region during the war with little success at regaining the state's loyalty. Educated free Blacks as well as Union military and political leaders, including Lincoln, dreamed of Louisiana becoming a model of reconstruction and progress but the secessionist majority fought them tooth and nail for control. In addition, rural Louisiana held "a larger class of slaveholding free Blacks than any other Southern state" and actually organized free Black militia companies with the onset of war.[18] After the war, "Louisiana became a unique epicenter of violent politics. This occurred, not because Louisiana was typical of the Old South, but precisely because it was so singularly distinct in its population, its geography, and the role it played in the conduct of the war." Unlike other Southern states, Louisiana contained a "large and vibrant" community of free Blacks.[19] In fact, New Orleans contained the "largest, the wealthiest, and the best-educated community of free Blacks in the country. Not even New York City could boast of having more...." By 1860, they had accumulated over $2 million worth of property.[20] New Orleans and Louisiana in general, played a distinctive role in Reconstruction politics with its strategic location near the mouth of the Mississippi and as a trading center.

Since the Union occupation in 1862, racial tension had been on the rise. One reason was General Benjamin Banks' decision to organize fugitive slaves into volunteer regiments.[21] The citizens of New Orleans, forced to "suffer" the double indignation of occupation by Union troops and Black soldiers, seethed with anger. This led to confrontations and unrest among the population and ultimately a vicious race riot on July 30, 1866. The United States Army was pulled into the center of this tumult.

Thrust into this roiling turmoil, 1st Lieutenant Henry Robinett arrived in New Orleans, ambitious as ever, optimistic about his future, and confident in his abilities. The 1st U.S. Infantry had elements stationed throughout the city including Jackson Barracks just outside the city.[22] Henry found himself posted inside the city near Lafayette Square at Lafayette and Camp Streets where his unit shared a building with a saloon and meeting hall.

Endnotes

1. Letters Received by the Commission of the Adjutant General's Office, 1863-1870; (National Archives Microfilm Publication M1064, Roll 106); 1864, M136 – M576.

2. Ibid.

3. Family Papers, October 4, 1864 letter to Theodore Robinett. Lou's husband would go on to serve in the 4th U.S. Infantry.

4. Reed, 26.

5. Ibid. 30.

6. OR. SERIES I--VOLUME XXXVII/1 [S# 70] p. 226.

7. See Steven Woodworth's "Nothing but Victory: The Army of the Tennessee, 1861 – 1865," Alfred A. Knopf, 2005 where he indicates Grant was biding his time waiting for a blatant act of insubordination before he would remove such a powerful political figure as McClernand. He was relieved of command by Grant on June 18 after publishing a letter in the press congratulating his corps after their assault of May 19-20 contrary to orders issued by Grant. Previously Woodworth indicates he had been working for Grants removal and spreading rumors concerning Grant's excessive drinking.

8. Simon, John Y. "The Papers of Ulysses S. Grant." Volume 11. June 1 – August 15, 1864. Carbondale, IL: Southern Illinois University Press, 1982, p. 455.
127. See Steven Woodworth's "Nothing but Victory: The Army of the Tennessee, 1861 – 1865," Alfred A. Knopf, 2005 where he indicates that was biding his

time waiting for a blatant act of insubordination before he would remove such a powerful political figure as McClernand. He was relieved of command by Grant on June 18 after publishing a letter in the press congratulating his corps after their assault of May 19-20 contrary to orders issued by Grant. Previously Woodworth indicates he had been working for Grants removal and spreading rumors concerning Grant's excessive drinking.

9. Family Papers, October 4, 1864 letter to Theodore Robinett.

10. Family Papers, February 6, 1865 letter to Theodore Robinett.

11. Family Papers, July 25, 1865 letter to Theodore Robinett.

12. Family Papers, February 6, 1865 letter to Theodore Robinett

13. Letters Received by the Commission of the Adjutant General's Office, 1863-1870; (National Archives Microfilm Publication M1064, Roll 125); 1865, S389—S597.

14. Family Papers, July 25, 1865 letter to Theodore Robinett.

15. Ibid.

16. There are a few studies of Louisiana and New Orleans during this period: Henry Clay Warmouth, "War, Politics, and Reconstruction: Stormy Days in Louisiana." Columbia, SC: University of South Carolina Press, 2006 [This is the memoirs of carpetbagger Warmouth who was elected governor in 1868 and eventually impeached in 1873.]. James G. Hollandsworth, Jr. "An Absolute Massacre: The New Orleans Race Riot of July 30, 1866." Baton Rouge, LA: Louisiana State University, 2001. James K. Hogue, "Uncivil War: Five New Orleans Street Battles and the Rise and Fall of Radical Reconstruction." Baton Rouge: Louisiana State University Press, 2006. Ted Tunnell, "Crucible of Reconstruction: War, Radicalism, and Race in Louisiana 1862-1877." Baton Rouge, LA: Louisiana State University, 1984. Each of these works presents interesting aspects of reconstruction New Orleans and the effect the stationing of United States troops had upon the citizenry.

17. Tunnell, 29.

18. Ibid. 69.

19. Hogue, 4.

20. Hollandsworth, 11.

21. Hollandsworth, 55.

22. "President Andrew Jackson signed a Congressional bill on July 19, 1832 that provided $87,000 for the building of a post to house U.S. troops. An additional $107,500 was appropriated by Congress bringing the total cost to over $180,000. The site for Jackson Barracks was purchased on December 16, 1833 from Pierre Cotteret. The area was chosen for its close proximity to the city and the four forts guarding it against a seaborne invasion like Jackson had faced here in 1815. The forts would be the first line of defense and the barracks would serve as the main supply and troop center, sending these things where most needed in the time of attack. A.B. Roman, governor of Louisiana, wanted the troops garrisoned in the city to discourage any possible slave uprisings but President Jackson wanted them away from the inner city and the "distrustful" Creole population, hence the present site was chosen as a compromise. Lieutenant Frederick Wilkinson, a 23 year old West Point graduate, designed and supervised the building of the barracks in February 24, 1834 until completion on December 31, 1835. The barracks was built on a 300 by 600 foot site which fronted the river. In addition to the fourteen original buildings which stand today there was a headquarters building and two guard towers which were identical to the two which remain today. The quadrangle design in the center of the post was designed to be a rallying point for the Louisiana volunteer militia to join along with the regulars in the event of attack. The barracks was known back then as New Orleans Barracks or simply U.S. Barracks. The first troops were in the barracks by February of 1837. Colonel David E. Twiggs was the first commandant of the Post, also serving as commanding officer of the 2nd Regiment of Dragoons. The first use that the barracks got was to serve as a temporary post for troops moving through LA to and from the Florida Seminole war in 1836. Indians who had made peace with the U.S. government were sent out West, but not before a brief stay at the Barracks while waiting for a ship to take them upriver. When Louisiana seceded in 1861, Louisiana militia units were there to take over the barracks. They took down the flag of the United States and raised the Pelican flag. The Confederacy used the post as a militia training center and retained control until April 1862, when Admiral David Farragut reclaimed the city for the Union. Farragut turned the post over to "Beast" Butler, and it remained a garrison for Union troops until well into the period of Reconstruction. Jackson Barracks: Building the U.S. Army Post. http://www.la.ngb.army.mil/dmh/jbm_jbhist.htm I would like to thank Colonel Tommy Ryan, Louisiana National Guard Historian for his assistance and the personal tour he conducted for me of the Barracks.

Chapter VI:
"School of the True Gentleman"

Trouble in New Orleans

The summer of 1865 was uneventful as Robinett settled into the unit's routine, but conflict and confrontation met him in November of 1865. His first unfortunate encounter occurred on November 10 while Henry was loading his baggage into a wagon and was stopped by Major Maurice Maloney, a long-time officer in the 1st U. S., having seen action with the unit throughout the war. Maloney was supervising the loading of a wagon when Henry approached and said, "I will put my baggage in the wagon." When the major informed him he could not, he repeated the statement and added, "I would like to catch any person putting it out." "Along with other words in a disrespectful manner." Major Maloney told Robinett he should consider himself under arrest and in the presence of both other officers and civilians Henry replied, "You are not my commanding officer. I will not respect your authority." Henry added, "You are a damned fool" or other words to that effect.[1] This is even more astonishing as Major Maloney commanded his unit at Corinth and Vicksburg. Maloney was commended for his actions at Vicksburg where his section of the 1st U.S. was involved in the action that became known as "The Crater."

Placed under arrest, Lieutenant Robinett was charged with "conduct prejudicial to good order and military discipline as well as using contemptuous and disrespectful language to his superior officer." Found guilty on both counts, Robinett was sentenced on

December 16 to suspension from rank, pay, and privileges for one month. The Assistance Adjutant General of the Gulf George Lee added:

The Major Commanding trusts that the rebuke given…will be sufficient warning to him of the enormity of his offense, and regrets that he should be obliged thus publicly to reprimand an officer of a Regiment of note for its discipline, for so gross an offence as disrespect to an officer greatly his senior, both in years, rank, and experience.[2]

Camp Street, New Orleans courtesy of Washington Artillery of New Orleans http://www.washingtonartillery.com/albumen,%20 Decatur%20St.jpg

This incident by itself might be considered a minor slip and the punishment certainly not great enough to bring too much discredit upon Robinett. Perhaps for a brief moment on Camp Street Robinett imagined his brevet rank still held some worth or maybe, though unlikely, he simply had a personality conflict from previous years with Maloney. Taken by itself, the case is of little consequence.

Yet, while this case was still under adjudication, an incident on Saturday, November 25 clearly demonstrated that something was amiss within Robinett. At approximately 5 P.M., Lieutenant Robinett entered the saloon owned by Andrew Kissinger adjacent to the post accompanied by two enlisted men from the regiment. Evidently, he had invited the two veterans, from another company and unknown to him before this encounter, in for a drink. Andrew Kessinger noted his entry into the establishment and then accompanied a visitor upstairs to tour the Odd Fellows Hall. According to Kissinger, Robinett appeared to be "a little under the influence of liquor." Henry Kessinger was in charge of the bar while his brother was upstairs. Henry had served in the Union army and talked to Robinett briefly about his service. Robinett asked for drinks and the bartender refused to serve him since he appeared intoxicated. Robinett then demanded to see the owner, and Henry Kessinger refused. Henry testified that he was going to serve the men but that Robinett said, "He could pull any man out from behind that bar that ever stood behind it." He also claimed Robinett took him by the arm after jumping over the bar and insisted he call his brother. At this time, Kessinger left to seek out the officer of the day.

The officer of the day was Captain Isaac Denniston DeRussy.[3] Captain DeRussy ordered the two enlisted men away, and it is here the stories diverge. DeRussy and Henry Kessinger claim Robinett said to the enlisted men, "You are not going to obey him, are you?" While Robinett testified that he said, "You are going to obey him, aren't you?" Neither of the men clearly heard what Robinett said. Both enlisted men felt that Lieutenant Robinett was intoxicated. Captain DeRussy claimed that when he asked Robinett to come outside, Robinett asked him if it was an order or a request. He considered Robinett's behavior was "calculated to prejudice his authority over said enlisted men and incite a mutinous spirit on their part." He also believed that Robinett was intoxicated. Robinett was placed under arrest and another court martial was scheduled for December. He was charged with "conduct unbecoming an officer and a gentleman, conduct to the prejudice of good order and military discipline, and inciting a mutinous spirit on the part of enlisted men in his regiment."[4]

A Mr. N. Bienvenue, a schoolteacher, testified that Robinett had been at his house from approximately 1 to 3 P.M. "talking the town" and that he was "perfectly sober or free from intoxication." Afterwards, Dr. S. Catlin, assistant surgeon for the 1st U.S., testified that Robinett was at his residence until just before 5 P.M. and that he did not think that the lieutenant was intoxicated. Two other civilians testified that Robinett did not appear intoxicated before the incident at the saloon. Something was obviously amiss if these gentlemen indicated he was not intoxicated while Kessinger and DeRussy felt he was.

Given the opportunity to write a defense rather than testify, Robinett wrote a rambling response beginning with perfect penmanship and ending with angry scrawls, heavy underlining, and numerous scribbles. In the beginning, he addressed the charge of mutiny with logic and reason based upon the testimony. He claimed that he could not be accused of inciting mutiny if the enlisted men did not behave or appear to be mutinous. He stated the men showed no disposition to mutiny and obeyed DeRussy; therefore, there was not mutinous spirit or "an open resistance to such authority." He also cited the fact that both enlisted men testified they did not hear him suggest they disobey the order to Captain DeRussy. Then he turned his attention to obeying DeRussy's order, "It might possibly have been and in all probability, was asked for information and without the least intent or desire to incite a mutinous spirit." He also stated it was not Captain DeRussy's responsibility to determine if his conduct was to incite mutiny but rather the courts. From this point on, his writing becomes angry. It contains numerous blots, smudges, and underlining, and his handwriting degenerates accordingly. He is clearly angry, more and more upset as he wrote.

Robinett claimed that there was no evidence, aside from Henry Kessinger's account, that he used force or behaved in an overtly aggressive manner. He also stated that since the unit had been quartered in the same building as the saloon for so long, numerous officers had "taken liberties" to move behind the bar and get their drinks themselves. Then he borders on the ridiculous by contending that when asking the enlisted men to have a drink with him, "it does not necessarily follow that a drink of liquor is intended…for it is courtesy to allow the person to whom this invitation is extended to choose for himself whether his beverage shall be Cold Sparkling Water, Ruby Wine, Lemon Ade, Soda or Bourbon or Cognac!" Besides, he continued, "There is no law which can punish any officer or enlisted man belonging to the army of the U.S., whether off or on duty, from drinking liquor; -- but there is a penalty awarded to each officer or soldier by the 45 Article of War for being drunk on duty."

Next he appealed to the court's patriotism in a bizarre fashion:

Remember, gentlemen, if you will, that the rebellion has scarcely closed, and how many fit associates for any men in our land, were during it found in the ranks of our army. Our relatives of every degree—our brothers: and in several instances, or occasions of great national danger, where the loyal north was invaded by Treason's minions-even our gray-haired and venerated fathers shouldered their musket and did noble service in defense of "the Government." And their homes and fire-sides! Shall we then bring such disgrace and odium on the name of the "American Soldiery"-those who have served during the whole of "the great rebellion" as well as many years before-by deciding that it is unbecoming an officer and gentleman to ask one of these veterans marked by many a seemy scar to ask to take a drink: for so doing us basely show our appreciation for their noble and heroic conduct in the service of their country and to sustain the dignity of government and the majesty of its laws!

If we are so inclined, and judgment in the sentence of the trial be unfavorably to the accused, what man among that noble class of hero-patriot-citizen or regular-soldier will accept that good old and time honored maxim as truth "Dulce et decorum est pro patria mori" [It is sweet and fitting to die for one's country]⁵ It smacks too much of the puffed and exclusive notions inculcated by the etiquette and customs of the "Aristocratical Service of European Despotism" to be so considered or decided.

The passage reads like the ramblings of a psychotic mind. One can only wonder how the officers of the court reacted to this homily. He ends this section with reference to his upbringing as a gentleman no doubt referring to Delaware Military Academy.

We have not the least desire to convince the Court that we would be accredited to that school of so-styled gentleman, known as the affected, popinjay and foppish: but we do and will claim for him that he belongs to the "School of the true gentleman":-for he never on any occasion forgets his early education; or the inculcations fixed indelibly upon his youthful mind at the domestic fire-side, where he was bred in the "true school of the Gentleman!"

It seems he was much more offended by the accusation of conduct unbecoming an officer and gentleman than by any other accusation made.

As to the charge of intoxication, his rant ended with, "It has not been shown, much less proven, by any one witness in his testimony that the accused was under the influence of extra ordinary exhilaration, delirium, or stupor, or was unable to articulate perfectly or govern voluntary motion generally".

Concluding his defense, he wrote:

It must be most evident to the Gentlemen of the Court Martial from the testimony of the case "in toto" that the Prosecution has entirely and signally failed to substantive the specifications to which any criminality can be attached and consequently both charges and specifications fall to the ground and in the consequence thereof and as a matter of course the accused has been wrongfully charged and must be acquitted for the whole.

The court ignored all of Robinett's sprawling appeal and found him guilty on all counts, dismissing him from service in the United States Army. Additionally, when the Judge Advocate General reviewed the case he wrote to Lieutenant General Grant:

> *It may be remarked that this officer had been tried but a short time before the trial which resulted in his dismissal, by the same Court ....and that his being soon brought again to trial, probably induced the severity of his sentence. It is for the Lieutenant General to decide whether the consideration of Lieut. Robinett's meritorious service during the war, which brought to his knowledge, can be deserved sufficient to call for his re-instatement in the service.*

What can we learn from these combined affairs about Henry Robinett and his world? The fact that the second one occurred before the first ended indicates a lack of self-control on Robinett's part. Most soldiers under charge would try exceptionally hard not to create another incident, yet Henry seemed to incite the second. He most definitely exhibited peculiar behavior at the Kessinger saloon and his confrontation with Captain DeRussy outside. The evidence clearly showed before arriving at the saloon he had not been drinking yet he did behave as if he was intoxicated. His behavior seems out of character with his past but it is obvious that something had altered his mental capacity. At this point, and certainly for the Army, it was obvious that his conduct was excessive and "outside the bounds of good order."[6] His commanding officer in New Orleans, Colonel Robert Buchanan wrote, "I cheerfully state that during that period (1865) he was always zealous and attentive to his duty and his conduct was such as to merit my approval." Lieutenant Robinett revealed a Jekyll/Hyde personality unnoticed until now.

Vindication and Return

Robinett's networking came into play as numerous powerful dignitaries stepped into these affairs. In February of

1866, General Rawlings, on behalf of Grant, wrote to General James Holt, the Adjutant General, asking that he examine the records and consider remission of the decision. Senator George R. Riddle wrote to Secretary of War, Edwin M. Stanton, on behalf of numerous Delaware dignitaries and the congressional delegation on April 7, 1866. He was not only seeking reinstatement but also promotion!

> *William Hall, the District Judge of Delaware for twenty five years, and many other prominent citizens of Delaware, have recommended Henry C. Robinett now a 1st Lieutenant in the Regular Army for promotion to a Majority...Mr. Robinett served five years in the Army, was severely wounded and, I think, is entitled to the commission. My opinion is that the Delaware delegation will be a unit in this case.*[7]

This is a remarkable letter since Robinett had been dismissed from service by this time. Henry's network of powerful friends was coming to his aid. On April 21, 1866, at General Grant's recommendation, his conviction was mitigated and he was ordered back to service on April 24th and by May 13th he had rejoined the 1st U.S. in New Orleans. Robinett's actions in these two incidents suggest some type of behavioral disorder, and his problems, though apparently resolved, had just begun.

Captain Robinett returned to New Orleans in May of 1866 and found the city little changed, full of racial turmoil and animosity towards the Yankee occupiers. The Louisiana Constitution of 1864 had given Blacks greater freedoms but not the right to vote. With President Johnson's amnesty proclamation of 1865 and the issuance of pardons brought almost all former Rebels back into the Union. Indeed, at the end of 1865, while Robinett was enduring the two courts martial, most of the Southern states were back under the control of the same type of men who had led them into war. Union sympathizers in Louisiana, thrown out of political office, watched as the recently elected state legislature enacted Black Codes to maintain order over the Freedmen.

In July of 1866, the adjourned convention of 1864, reconvened at the Mechanics' Institute in New Orleans while an angry white crowd gathered outside. In the streets, black supporters of the convention, which was to discuss enfranchising the Freedmen, shoved their way through the throng and exchanged angry words with the mob. Shots rang out and the confrontation rapidly degenerated into a riot.

In all likelihood, Captain Robinett was involved in suppressing the riot but he never comments about it in his few letters from the period. He must have been aware of the raw nerves on both sides, the animosity, and the distain most Louisianans held for the U.S. Army. His unit, now removed to Jackson Barracks, was just three miles from the city proper and was on alert that Monday, prepared to move into the city. In addition, the 81st Infantry, U.S. Colored Troops was also available.[8] Several companies of the 1st U.S. were ordered into the city just after noon. In the aftermath, General Sheridan ordered the 1st U.S. to remain in Lafayette Square along with an artillery battery. In a preliminary report to President Johnson one week later he wrote:

> *The immediate cause of this terrible affair was the assemblage of this Convention. The remote cause was the bitter and antagonistic feeling which has been growing in this community since the advent of the present mayor, who in the organization of the police force selected many desperate men, and some of them known murderers....It is useless to attempt to disguise the hostility that exists on the part of a great many here towards northern men, and this unfortunate affair has so precipitated matters that there is now a test of what shall be the status of northern men.*[9]

The 1st U.S. and other Army units were called in to subdue the crowd but not until forty-eight men were dead and over two hundred wounded.[10] "The New Orleans riot ignited a new conflict that raged for more than a decade and thus became to the second phase of the Civil War what Fort Sumter was to the first.[11] Unreconstructed Confederate John T. Monroe, elected mayor, removed all Unionists from the city's police force replacing them with former Confederate soldiers and sympathizers.

Captain Henry C. Robinett was about to propel himself headlong into this maelstrom of "bitter, desperate, and hostile men."

Endnotes

1. Letters Received by the Commission of the Adjutant General's Office, 1863-1870; (National Archives Microfilm Publication M1064, Roll 121); 1865, R755 – R919.

2. Ibid.

3. "Isaac D. DeRussy was born in 1840 at Fort Monroe, Virginia. He began his service as a Second Lieutenant with the 1st United States Infantry and by the end of the Civil War was a Captain. He participated in the siege of Corinth in May and June of 1862 and was brevetted Major in 1865 for faithful and meritorious service during the war. He also served with the 4th, 14th and 11th United States Infantry regiments. While commanding the 11th regiment as a Colonel, he also commanded Fort Huachuca, Arizona, in 1891 and 1892. On 10 August 1898 he led his regiment against Spanish forces near Hormiguero, Puerto Rico. He was retired on 1 April 1902 as a brigadier general and died on 17 February 1923 in New York City. He was buried in Section 3 of Arlington National Cemetery." http://www.arlingtoncemetery.net/idderussy.htm.

4. The complete transcript and supporting documents for the Robinett's second court martial are here: Records of the Office of the Judge Advocate General Court Martial Case Files, 1809-1894; (National Archives Record Group 153, File MM-3435.

5. Dulce et decorum est pro patria mori is a line from the Roman poet Horace's Odes (III.2.13).

Dulce et decorum est pro patria mori:
How sweet and fitting it is to die for one's country:
mors et fugacem persequitur virum
Death pursues the man who flees,
nec parcit inbellis iuventae
Spares not the hamstrings or cowardly backs
poplitibus timidove tergo.
Of battle-shy youths.

The phrase can be found at the front entrance to the Arlington Memorial Amphitheater at the Arlington National Cemetery. It is also found on the second monument of the Point Lookout Confederate Cemetery in Point Lookout, MD, and at the Confederate Cemetery in the Manassas Battlefield National Park.

6. Records of the Office of the Judge Advocate General Court Martial Case Files, 1809-1894; (National Archives Record Group 153, File MM-3435.

7. Letters Received by the Commission of the Adjutant General's Office, 1863-1870; (National Archives Microfilm Publication M1064, Roll 129); 1866, R5—R364.

8. Sheridan to Andrew Johnson, August 6, 1866, in Philip Sheridan Papers, container 52, reel 47, pp. 415-20. Found in Hollandsworth, 144-5.

9. See James G. Hollandsworth, Jr. "An Absolute Massacre: The New Orleans Race Riot of July 30, 1866." Baton Rouge, LA: Louisiana State University, 2001.

10. Ibid. p 3.

11. Ibid. 72.

Chapter VII:
A Boston Red Sox Fan in Yankee Stadium

Robinett's return to New Orleans and the 1st U.S. Infantry was uneventful through the summer and into fall. On Wednesday, October 13, 1866, Henry Robinett found himself off duty and with time on his hands. Around 7 P.M., Robinett called upon 1st Lieutenant John W. Purcell, a member of his regiment, and Purcell's wife at their residence in New Orleans. He had a glass of wine, conversed for about a half an hour, and then asked Purcell if he would lend him a dollar so he could see the show at the Varieties Theatre. Purcell lent him three.[1] Lieutenant Purcell recalled, "I think he was perfectly sober and able to take care of himself, he conducted himself as a gentleman so and as I saw him."[2]

Photographer John H. Clark saw Henry on Canal Street near the door to the theatre standing on the banquette[3] in front of the Theatre around 8 P.M. and talked to him for about a half hour. "I don't say that he was drunk, he had probably been drinking. I think he took a drink with me. I think he was sober and knew what he was about. He appeared to be very cool."

Mr. Joseph P. Chandler, steamboat clerk and captain on the river, met Robinett at the ticket office and they went into the parquette[4] together when a confrontation occurred.

These gentlemen made some remarks to him [Robinett] which I thought very uncalled for and we continued to stand there for some moments. My state pride was aroused and I said come and go down to the banquette and see what they want and I think that on that occasion the conduct of the accused was that of an officer and a gentleman. They (crowd) applied some epithets and he

[Robinett] acted very cool and calm in the whole proceeding he was very forbearing. He was a little under the influence I admit, but not anything that anyone could take exceptions to. He had been drinking and was friendly; he was what I should call affectionately drunk. He did not wish to fight and wished to avoid anything.

Varieties Theatre - courtesy of http://www.angelpig.com/storyville/neworleans.html

Captain S. H. Warren, a white officer in the 116th U.S. Colored Infantry attended the performances that evening. He recalled hearing, "Come on down here you are just my man!" and Robinett replied, "Oh no Sir, I don't want to fight or have any quarrel" with the crowd and Robinett went out onto the street. "He had the appearance of being perfectly sane and sensible and of being perfectly gentlemanly. The idea of him being intoxicated did not enter my mind."

Mr. Stephen Wilkins, a clerk, witnessed the affair outside the Theater. He saw Captain Robinett in an animated conversation with some citizens, "I think he was sober, I did not see him do anything ungentlemanly at that time." At this point, the incident was resolved peacefully and Robinett returned to the Theatre where he sat in the orchestra chairs for the evening's performances of "Romeo & Juliet" and "The Farce." From here, the accounts vary.

According to Robinett, he enjoyed the shows and no issues of note arose until the end of the third act when an usher, a police officer, and an angry mob of theatergoers accosted him, roughly handling him and took him out of the theatre. First Lieutenant Frank R. Chase in the 18th Veteran Reserve Corps was also in the theater. He first noticed Captain Robinett "by hearing him cry 'encore' and clapping his hands, this was at the time of a general applause by the audience." A short time later he did the same thing when an usher came and spoke to Robinett. The third time Robinett cheered the performance, an usher "took hold of the lapel of his coat as if he was going to pull him out, the usher went back out and then returned and took hold of the lapel of the [Robinett's] coat again, as if to pull him out and gave him a jerk. Then let go and turned away." A third usher came along and grabbed Robinett and "took hold of him and they pulled him off." Three or four of the audience yelled, "Pull him out!" One or two said, "Put out the damned Yankee!" Robinett, according to Chase said, "Gentleman do not make any disturbance. If you want me to go out I will go out peacefully." Chase saw Lieutenant Spaulding go to Robinett's aid, trying to get the crowd to leave him alone and tried to pull him out of the theatre backwards. "I also saw two or three persons strike at him. I saw the glisten of some weapon, apparently a knife." Down the stairs he heard someone exclaim, "He had got one good crack at the damned Yankee at any rate!"

Second Lieutenant Spaulding remembered, "I saw Captain Robinett surrounded by quite a crowd of men who were attempting to put him out. He was telling them, 'Let me alone and I will go out, but you cannot force me out!' He told the crowd to let him go and he would take him out but they continued to drag him out and Spaulding went back to get Robinett's cap on the ground."

F. J. Hyatt, a New Orleans police officer told a completely different tale.

In the early part of the evening the accused had a difficulty with Mr. Charles Adams, as to what the nature....I don't know....I was up in the theatre and I heard of the difficulty. I went down on the banquette in front of the theatre and I then saw a large crowd collecting in the front of the door, and as I am responsible for all difficulties that occur in that theatre I did not wish to have any difficulty there and I requested a watchman to take the accused, who was not in my opinion perfectly sober, down to the corner, which he did. Some time (maybe an hour or so) elapsed and some gentleman came to me and told me that several ladies had had to leave the Theatre on account of the annoyance of some gentleman down in the briquette and requested me to go down and speak to him. I sent one of his aides to handle the affair. After the first act some gentleman came again and requested me to have the noise stopped or the party taken out of the Theatre. I sent two men down to the gentleman.

Then Hyatt decided to go down and investigate himself,

I heard the accused making a noise and talking to actors on the Stage (Mr. Pierson who was singing, he said, "Go it old fellow" or "bully for you" in a loud voice so as to attract the attention of the entire audience... I myself requested the accused to be quiet or leave - and received no answer - I had, with the assistance of two police officers, to eject him from the Theatre. After a great deal of resistance on the part of the accused we got him out of the Theatre and when I got him out of the Theatre I turned him over to the watchman in front of the Theatre and told him to take him to the Chief of Police. One of the parties who requested me to put him out was a federal officer in uniform who said that he ought to have been put out and hour ago."

Hyatt was a former Confederate Army officer.

The actor on stage at the time, Harry Pierson, played a piece called "Fortune's Frolic" and sang two songs. He heard no disturbance while on stage, and indicated his performance was not interrupted "in the slightest" by the actions of Captain Robinett.

Another police officer, J. P. Champaign, remembered, "I went down and did not see anyone making any fuss at the time." He heard more commotion, went back to the orchestra chairs, and sat behind Robinett. "I asked him if he would not be so kind as to step to the back part of the house with me, he said, 'No, he would not, he would not stir for no man except Mr. King.' To the best of my knowledge the accused was under the influence of liquor." Robinett, according to Champaign, "clapped his hands louder than he ought to do." Supposedly, the ladies in front of Robinett left, and the officer "Took hold of the accused, cries were being raised from the different parts of the house 'take him out.' He [Robinett] was hollering and clapping his hands in a boisterous manner and calculated to disturb the audience in the Theatre." He continued, "I think that a sober man when corrected for making a disturbance in a theatre would remain quiet, and a drunken man would only repeat the offense. I did not strike the accused with a mace or what is commonly called a 'Billy' and did not hear 'Put out the Yankee Son of a Bitch.' Officer Hyatt served one year in the Confederate Army during the war."

Mr. Thomas Flanagan, clerk and usher at Variety Theatre, believed Robinett was yelling, "Bravo, Bravo" and clapping his hands loudly. He asked him to stop, and Robinett indicated he would. However, according to Flanagan, Robinett repeated the noise, and Flanagan went for police. Flanagan claimed that Robinett stated, "That he was there by orders from King and would not leave until King gave him orders to leave."[5] Flanagan did not hear any offensive language. "He did not act like a sober man but I could not positively say whether the accused was intoxicated or not, but in my opinion, I think the accused was rather under the influence of liquor." Mr. Henry St. Germain, treasurer of the Varieties Theatre, said he ordered Robinett removed if the usher thought noise was unbecoming.

Mr. S.W. Pescary, a cotton warehouseman, attended the show that night, "I turned around, I was three rows in front of Robinett, and saw a crowd apparently taking someone out." He indicated there was no disturbance before that. Mr. J. L Winslow, a cotton factor,[6] saw Robinett in the theatre, "The usher and two or three of the gentlemen sitting near took the accused out of the Theatre by force." He believed the conduct of Captain Robinett was "very gentlemanly" and "saw no cause for it (violence) whatever. He resisted the ushers and I heard him make a remark as he got to the head of the stairs, that he was a Major (or I am a Mason) and that if they would let him alone he would go out."[7]

Lieutenant Colonel J. L. Haskell heard Robinett saying that if they would just release him he would go out of the Theatre. He estimated one-half to one-third of the audience joined the crowd. Haskell did not previously notice anything to disturb the performance, and he believed the use of force was "all together unnecessary." Robinett, he noted, was "excited and not from liquor" and that "The majority of the men left on account of a United States Officer being ejected from the Theater." He indicated Captain Robinett was "not, in my opinion, drunk at any time, though I had no way of telling." He also stated that besides Robinett there was one other officer in uniform in the Theatre, Lieutenant Hamilton. Brevet Lieutenant Colonel J. Strang, Quartermaster, was at the Theatre and indicated four or five people grabbed Robinett who exclaimed, "Gentleman why this force? If you wish me to go out I will go out as a gentleman."

Mr. S.A. Freeman, a surgeon's steward on the Iron clad Fleet, berthed in Algiers near New Orleans heard, "Put him out" five of six seats behind him but that was the extent of the disturbance. J.B. Reynor, mate in the U.S. Navy, was at Theatre and heard "Put him out" followed by "let me alone, I am a gentleman, I will go out by myself." He indicated that he saw nothing in Robinett's behavior unbecoming an officer. "I don't think he would have been ejected if he was a citizen. Because I did not hear or see anything that would justify anyone in being put out and I know the feeling that exists in this city towards Army officers."

Later, Daniel McLean, a physician, said Robinett showed him his hand, "It was a wound as if it had been a bite, there was a wound on each side of the hand showing that it had been pressed between two hard substances." He also said, "I have known Captain Robinett for over one year and believe him to be of an excitable temperament. I have seen him under the influence of liquor and he is still more excitable under such circumstance."

After Robinett was forcibly expelled from the Theatre, Robinett was "handed to [Officer J. L. Holmes] to take him to the Station House under arrest on Gravier Street, in front of the Varieties Theatre, about 10 o'clock." and was ordered to charge him with disturbing the peace of the theatre. "He [Robinett] was a little excited, showed blood on his hand, and said that he had been abused. He seemed to be excited from being abused. I should have been apt to have noticed it. [If he was intoxicated] He showed every appearance to be a gentleman. He walked straight enough but talked rather excited as if from being abused." Colonel Thomas A. Adams, the Chief of Police, said Robinett was brought to his headquarters between ten and eleven P.M. by "affectionately tight means" and charged with intoxication and disturbing the peace. From there, escorted to Army headquarters on Lafayette Square, Robinett would encounter his old nemesis, Captain DeRussy.

Colonel Adams woke DeRussy sometime between 11 P.M. and midnight and informed him Captain Robinett was crying drunk. When he arose and went outside, he saw Robinett "crying outside the tent and talking in a discomforting manner. He was talking in a very boisterous manner to some gentlemen who were with him, making such a disturbance that the Sentinel on post then called for the Corporal of the guard." According to DeRussy, he told Robinett not to make so much noise in camp and Robinett responded, "Go to Hell!" and walked off. DeRussy ordered him to leave his camp, but Captain Robinett became more abusive.

"God damn him, he [DeRussy] is no soldier! He is a sycophant," Robinett exclaimed. After more commotion, Robinett was taken to the headquarters of General Sheridan. According to Captain DeRussy, Robinett "seemed very much intoxicated." Robinett returned thirty minutes later, went into some of the men's tents, and shouted, "Are you all dead in here?" DeRussy claimed Robinett could not walk nor talk and was "very much under the influence."

Sergeant James P. Capron, of Company A, 1st U.S. Infantry, was in charge of guard at the camp and it was he who took the Chief of Police into the tent of DeRussy. "It (the peace of camp) was disturbed by loud talking around Capt. DeRussy's tent." He did not believe any of the men were actually disturbed because, "I did not see any of them out of their tents." Private James Will was on guard at post number 3 and heard DeRussy tell Robinett to "keep still" and Robinett say he would not. DeRussy, according to Will, said, "He [Robinett] was no gentleman." Half an hour later, Robinett returned to the camp. However, he did not notice any disturbance of the peace. According to Will, Robinett "spoke intelligently and reasonably and walked erect and straight like a sober man." He also did not hear him tell DeRussy to "Go to Hell" but heard him call him a sycophant. "He told him [DeRussy] that if he would come outside, he would shoot him through the heart, I believe. He acted as if he was excited or angry."

Second Lieutenant Spaulding accompanied Robinett from the theatre and felt "His behavior was that of a man laboring under excitement." He also remembered hearing Robinett say at the camp, "Go to Hell!" He believed that Robinett was under the influence of liquor and heard Robinett say, "If you come out here I will shoot you through the heart." Spaulding indicated that Robinett's "thumb of his left hand had the appearance of having been bitten."

First Lieutenant Frank Chase also went to DeRussy's camp and saw Robinett in an excited state. He recalled hearing him say to the Chief of Police, "I have been as good a friend as the police have ever had and now they treat me so damned shamefully, Andrew Johnson shall hear of this and I'll telegraph to General

Grant before tomorrow night. General Grant is a friend of mine, I have fought with him and he will not see me abused like this." He felt Robinett seemed very angry with DeRussy and heard him say, "Captain DeRussy had misused him and was always making against him and that he was no gentleman." Robinett also shouted at him, "I would not be a damned sycophant like you, I would die first." Chase tried to get Robinett to leave the camp with him but he would not. Later Chase did convince him to go back and beg DeRussy's pardon, as did the Chief of Police.

Captain DeRussy said Robinett, "Came to me the following day and asked me if I had informed Colonel Wood [his commanding officer] that he had been locked up in the Station house all night and that he had acted disgracefully at the Theatre." DeRussy said he had talked to Colonel Wood and that Wood already knew of the incident. At which point Robinett replied, "Someone had informed Colonel Wood that he had been locked up all night in the calaboose which he expressed it was a damned lie." He also admitted that Robinett said if he had acted improperly towards him that it was under excitement and that he would apologize. "It was not exactly an apology. It was not as I considered a total apology and was said in rather a defiant manner. It did not palliate anything that had taken place."

When DeRussy was asked, "Have not yourself and the accused had several differences during the past year of a personal nature and otherwise that would prevent the existence of the most friendly relations between the accused and yourself?" He replied, "No difference at all of a personal or social nature. The conduct of Captain Robinett was decidedly unbecoming an officer, the matter of preferring charges was something I intended to leave subject to the Regimental Commander." DeRussy either did not recall their previous encounter a year before at the Kessinger tavern or was under the impression that bygones be bygones; unless of course, he was lying. Captain Kimzie Bates indicated, "A coolness existed between them for some time. This summer I supposed that all difficulty had ceased as I have seen Captain Robinett a visitor at Captain DeRussy's tent and I supposed the whole affair [The previous Court Martial/ tavern incident] had died out. Captain DeRussy said to me when Captain Robinett was reinstated that he should forget all and welcome him back to the regiment." Yet First Lieutenant W. N. Tisdale recalled, "I have recollection of a coolness existing between Captain DeRussy and the accused about a year ago resulting from some words they had together in the Suttlers Store." Within days, Captain Robinett was formally placed under charge:

> *While in a state of intoxication did behave in a manner so unbecoming (as to disrupt and annoy the audience and actors in the said theater); and when requested by the usher and police officer in attendance to desist from such conduct, did persist in making a disturbance (and did use loud and insulting language to said usher and police-officer), and did continue to behave in such an unbecoming manner (as to interrupt the performance on the stage) and to cause the said usher and police-officer to forcibly eject him from the said theatre, and to take him as a prisoner to the First District police station.*

He was about to undergo his third court martial in less than a year.

After all the testimony, Robinett was again afforded the opportunity to write a defense and produced a much more thoughtful, rational piece without the incoherent ramblings and anger of his pervious defense. He begins, as if he knew his position was tenuous: "In Order to fully comprehend the Consequence of Your decision in such a case, particularly if it be unfavorable to the accused, you must first know the Approximate value and price of a Soldier's honor! A Soldier is the only man of all men, who feels himself rich indeed, When all but life and honor's lost!"[8] He continues:

> *The mercenary wretch, when conscious that honor no longer abides with him, consoles himself with the enormity of his ill gotten gain- the prince, to him, of that priceless gem, which the good and great men of all ages have held for about the Common things of life-about*

*fame principality and power! The merchant prizes above all things
else his merchandizing, the Lawyer his legal boon. The Physician,
his skill; but to the Soldier All things Else sinks into insignificance
in comparison with his honor! Now, gentlemen, despise the soldier
who has Sustained his own and his Country's honor on more
than one hard and desperately fought-field of battle-learning the
evidence of his devotion to Country and of his own heroism to
which the battle plain-of his hard earned reputation by degrading
him; strip him of all his well earned-honor and his Soldierly pride,
by passing a sentence in severity greater than the criminality of the
Offense "per se," would justify. Then you send back to "civil society"
a person who, if not forever afterwards deprived of his honor....By
sentencing away his character as an officer, and his future history,
whatever it may be, that time can never efface! You take from him
a Soldier's All - his honor.⁹*

He further indicated that the affair at the Varieties Theatre was
"a sheer and wanton violation of the rights of a Gentleman, and
stamps it as an uncalled for, brutal, outrageous, and Cowardly, and
shameful attack upon an Officer of the United States Army, as such,
the incentive to such an outrage, and the cause of the perpetration
thereof, being the deeply rooted prejudices engendered in the bitter
five Years War of Rebellion of the Southern States."

Captain Robinett also alluded to his now apparent mental
difficulties and excitability.

*...it is well known to Several members of the Court, some
acquainted with the accused for three years, That he is liable to
violent mental excitement under peculiar circumstances and
particularly when an insult or offense is offered to him, or an
injury or wrong is attempted to be perpetrated upon him. You will
not permit yourselves to construe this array of facts into a mere
extenuation, but in the name of justice and right you will decide a
sufficient excuse for any injured or insult on the part of the accused
towards Capt. DeRussy.*

Henry was well aware he had several psychological issues but was not sure where they originated nor how they could be resolved.

It is clearly shown…that the accused was laboring under a high state of mental excitement. Under and by the brutal, unhuman, cowardly and shameful treatment he received…Treatment that would have almost made frantic and maddening with anger any gentleman who possessed the spirit worthy of a Soldier! What true man, what Soldier, we ask, would brave the indignities and insults offered to and the outrage perpetrated upon the person of the accused.…and in consequence - of have been almost bordering upon madness itself.…those who are so high-spirited and repellant in their natures that they cannot brook with indifference an affront or shameful and disgraceful indignity, but who loose entire control of that Devil-attribute of our nation-passion-and there commit acts which others of a cooler and more phlegmatic nature would never be guilty of.

Clearly, he believed that he was a victim of circumstances brought on by the deep-seated hatred engendered by the War, the mood of Southern citizenry, and the recent events in New Orleans. He picked apart the testimony of the prosecution's witness with constant references to honor and truth. Concluding his defense, he reminded the court of his service in the War and listing all of the engagements in which he participated as well as his citations for gallantry at Corinth and Vicksburg. He made sure his last comments recounted his "close" relationship with his "friend" General Grant. All of this to no avail, found guilty on all counts, Major General Sheridan took action upon the case, dismissing Robinett from service. "This being the second time within the year…, sentenced to dismissal for the same offense, I cannot recommend a revocation or mitigation of his sentence."

However, yet again, this was not to be the end of the affair. A letter from the Bureau of Military Justice to the Secretary of War indicated, "a more lenient opinion in reference to conduct of Capt

Robinett" was justified and detailed the situation as seen by the Judge Advocate General Holt (Italics are mine):

1. *Before entering theater he appeared to have been assaulted or at least greatly insulted by a variety of individuals in the street.* The nature of this difficulty does not initially appear, though the inference is that his position in the army led to the insults by his assailants.

2. Entering the theatre the accused took his seat in the orchestra chairs close to the Circle and his chief if not lonely offense seems to have been the somewhat too uproarious expectation of his approval of the performance, and this too only when the rest of the audience were applauding also.

3. Several witnesses present at the time, including the actors on the stage, testify that they were not conscious of any undue disturbance until their attention was distracted to the forcible removal of the accused from the theatre.

4. *His ejection appears to have been accomplished with unnecessary violence, his hand being bitten, and his head receiving a severe blow not withstanding his offer to go out without assistance if the police would let him alone. His removal was accompanied by cries from portions of the audience of "Put out the damned Yankee!" Several witness testify that in their opinion if the offender had been a civilian he would not have been ejected, and no notice would have been taken of his conduct.*

5. On being taken to the Police Headquarters, he was at once sent by the Chief of the camp of one of the Companies of his regiment and delivered to Capt. DeRussy, commanding the detachment. *This officer refused to receive him, and as the Accused under the double stimulus of anger and drink, was loud and hysterical in his talk,* requested him to be quiet as he was disturbing the camp. The accused made some angry reply as Capt. DeRussy testified, told him to go to Hell. Other witnesses then present assent however that the accused did not make use of this expression, till after he had been told by them there that he asked an apology to Capt. DeRussy and had been ordered

out of his tent when he returned there then to express his regret for what he had said and done. He was then taken to Gen Sheridan's Headquarters.

6. *It is manifested throughout the case that ill-feeling on the part of the audience and police towards officers of the U.S. Army, had much to do with the disturbance in which the Accused found himself involved. It is clear however that the partial intoxication of Capt. Robinett left him into acts which he would not have committed in a sober state,* and which furnished such excuse for his summary and disgraceful expressions. His loud and discommunicative and violent and abusive demeanor at the camp of Capt. De Russy, moreover, cannot be regarded as otherwise than discreditable, though it is easy to believe that the exasperation caused by his insulting and scandalous treatment at the Theatre but just half hour before, had not had time to cool.

7. That he was dealt with by the city police and ushers of the theatre. *Several of which testify that they had served in the rebel army during the war, with uncalled for harshness, a study of the evidence makes clear and the outrage to which he was there subjected account in great degree for the excitement and rudeness of his manner in the camp of Capt. DeRussy.*

8. The Bureau feels great diffidence in adopting an opinion different in any degree from that held by the distinguished officer in command of the Dept. of the Gulf....which justify it in expressing a more lenient opinion in reference to the conduct of Capt. Robinett, than Gen Sheridan has believed it to be his duty to do. *The first specification seems scarcely to warrant, it is thought a conviction under the charge of conduct unbecoming an officer and gentleman.* With the exception of the allegation of partial drunkenness, the Court have eliminated; and an examination of the testimony shows very properly in every charge of such misconduct in Accused's past as should make him amenable to a conviction and punishment under this charge. And partial drunkenness is itself, although disgraceful and improper and deserving punishment, is not necessarily an offence so grievous as to call for the server penalty consequent

upon a violation of the 45th or the 83rd Article of War....*Capt. Robinett seems, while off duty, to have indulged in an expression of applause to a degree which in conjunction with the Uniform he wore, gave offence to certain ushers and policemen attached to the Variety Theatre*...the accused justified in applauding the performance, whereupon the police ejected him with needless violence and cruelty from the building....it is not seen that he can be properly accused of such conduct and under circumstances of great aggravation, of conduct unbecoming an officer and a gentleman.

9. The accused conduct towards Capt. DeRussy would have been more appropriately noticed in a charge alleging a break of the 99th article. Taken by the police to the camp of a brother officer of equal rank into himself while smarting under a sudden outrage and ill-treatment, he was ordered by Capt. DeRussy to cease to disrupt his camp, and replied where voluntary an apology for his words spoken at the moment of great excitement....There would seem to be nothing in the acts of Capt. Robinett as justification in the evidence which should be regarded as justly disgracing him in the eyes of his brother officer or as anything more than the angry retort of an equal, excited to fury by such undeserved indignities and anguish by the indifference of one from whom he had the right to expect at least a degree of sympathy. That he should have permitted himself to fall under the influence of liquor ... is an offense for which he doubtfully deserves punishment; but the circumstances of his case are such as to warrant the opinion, it is thought, that he does not merit the ruinous punishment...*it is regarded an error in judgment to have brought him to trial.* It is therefore respectfully advised that the sentence be mitigated to suspension from rank and pay for a limited period.[10]

The unemotional, detached assessment of those in Washington D.C. was far more accurate than the court or General Sheridan's opinion. The mood of the citizenry and the color of his uniform, no doubt, exasperated the situation. Clearly,

Robinett lost control while at DeRussy's camp. Indeed, due to their past relationship, taking him to that particular camp must have felt like pouring salt into his wounds. However, with three courts martial in under a year, one can understand the willingness of the Department of the Gulf and General Sheridan to believe that Robinett was totally at fault. There was obviously something psychologically wrong with Captain Robinett, something the Army had yet to recognize and, in spite of evidence to the contrary, the Army attributed to some level of intoxication. Truly, Captain Robinett was a "Boston Red Sox fan in Yankee Stadium" and did realize his actions might bring about a hostile reaction from the Rebels in the audience.

Endnotes

1. The Varieties Theatre was one of the most important playhouses in New Orleans also known as Placide's "Varieties," which stood on Gravier, between Carondelet and Baronne, near the site of the present Cotton Exchange. Varieties Alley still preserves its name. The house opened in 1849 under the management of Tom Placide, who was himself an actor, and not infrequently took part in the plays that he produced. Built by an association known as the "Varieties Club," which came into existence in 1849, and was connected with another dramatic club, the Histrionics, the origin of which has been traced back as far as the year 1840. The theater burned in 1854 and was rebuilt the next year, opening under the management of Dion Boucicault, who called it "The Gaiety." It regained its old name and burned again in 1870. The proprietors now changed the location of their theater, purchasing land in Canal Street and Dauphine, where the Maison Blanche now stands.
http://penelope.uchicago.edu/Thayer/E/Gazetteer/Places/America/United_States/Louisiana/New_Orleans/_Texts/KENHNO/45*.html

2. Records of the Office of the Judge Advocate General Court Martial Case Files, 1809-1894; (National Archives Record Group 153, File OO-1898.

3. A banquette is boardwalk in this case running in front of the Theatre.

4. The parquette is the main floor of a theater.

5. No one else mentions this and there is no indication as to whom this King might be.

6. Cotton planters relied on cotton factors (sometimes also called commission merchants) to sell their crops for them.

7. With his arms restrained, Robinett was probably trying to signal any other Freemasons in the audience for help.

8. Robinett quotes from "After The Battle," by Sir Thomas Moore.

9. Records of the Office of the Judge Advocate General Court Martial Case Files, 1809-1894; (National Archives Record Group 153, File OO-1898.

10. Ibid.

Chapter VIII:
"I have triumphed most gloriously over my enemies."

Dishonored and Disgraced

Disgraced, Henry returned to Wilmington and was assaulted with more bad news, "My little lady love, Elsie is quite ill indeed. Lou thinks she has little chance of recovering. I feel quite sad indeed about it, but still have strong hopes of her recovering." While home, Robinett sought the council of his family and, once again, called upon his powerful friends for assistance. Henry's father went to see Senator Willard Saulsbury and Congressman John Nicholson and according to Henry, they took "great interest in my case."[1] Henry wrote letters to both men and the Senator visited President Johnson three times about his case. This influence had great effect: fellow Freemason Andrew Johnson remitted his sentence in January of 1867, just one month after the court had adjourned. By February of 1867, Henry was back with the 1st U.S. Infantry with a surprise for his unit.

So you see I am just as I was before the trial with these exceptions, when it commenced I was only a 1st Lieutenant in my regiment. Now I am a full Captain in my own regiment and a "Brevet" Major in the U.S. Army. I have two Brevet Commissions, one of Captain and one of Major. Both bestowed for "gallant and meritous services" – one for the "Battle of Corinth" and the other for the "Siege of Vicksburg." My Brevet Captain's Commission dates back to Oct 4, 1862, and my Brevet Major's Commission dates back to July 4, 1863. So I can take rank, as Major, back more than three years.

Major Henry C. Robinett now felt he outranked Captain DeRussy, though the rank was a brevet dating from the war, and he certainly believed rightfully vindicated; yet he was bothered deeply that his honor was questioned. Robinett seemed ecstatic as he wrote to his brother Theodore from New Orleans in February of 1867:

> *I was the persecuted of a set of military tyrants and mean, unprincipled, and envious beings, miscalled men and gentlemen.... They brought the old charge of last Winter against me. Because, (I know of no other reason; there was certainly no just cause or occasion for it) if found guilty of it, they could get rid of me, and ruin me in a military way. The charge against me was based upon, firstly, a difficulty I unexpectedly and unintentionally got into at a Theatre in this city....You see I have triumphed most gloriously over my enemies. I imagine they will be satisfied to 'let me alone' and "Keep hands off" while Andrew Johnson is President anyhow. He is a just, fair man, and a noble patriot. I have ever had the fullest confidence in his fairness, justices and patriotism, and I now admire him more than ever before. He is true and just to all. I am only too sorry that there are so few noble specimens of such good, great, just and wise men in public and high positions in the country. If such were the case we would have been 'at peace' when the rebel armies surrendered to our Great General Grant.*

His deep-seated animosity towards his "enemies" is apparent, as is his respect for his newfound benefactor and Freemason brother, Andrew Johnson.

He also had a few sharp comments for DeRussy, "His treatment of me being so unbecoming a brother officer and a gentleman -- I told him to 'go to Hell.' I was so aggravated I also told him he was no soldier and he was not a gentleman. During the war he was on 'fancy duty.' He did not serve a 'single day in the field' with his regiment." This is not completely accurate as Isaac D. DeRussy was with the 1st U.S. Infantry during the Union siege of Corinth in May and June of 1862.

And what of the crowd at the Theatre?

...when it was perceived by some cut-throat thugs and "roughs" that I was an officer of the Army, a cry of "put him out", "put out the damned Yankee", and, I think, I heard cries also of "put out the damned Yankee Son-of-a bitch." These, I think, were the friends of a low fellow that I accidentally and unavoidably had gotten into a difficulty with earlier on the same night. Three ushers took hold of me in a rough and most violent manner, and followed and assisted by 50 or 100 of the rowdy element of the audience, attempted in a most brutal and uncalled for manner to eject me from the Theatre; to all of which, I, of course, being possed (sic) of a little courage and manhood and some little strength, and at such activity objected in a most serious and belligerent (sic) manner; knocking down and scattering sundry larger individuals than myself, much to their grief and astonishment.

Proud of the way he handled the incident and happy that things worked out in his favor, he was no doubt gloating over the failure of "his enemies" to bring him down. From this point forward, Robinett was comfortable in his rank and position as well as how these events were resolved.

In April, he received the news he hoped would not come. Elsie Sherwood Starr died on April 16, 1867, devastating Henry. She was the only woman he ever mentioned in his letters, his only love. He may have returned home for her funeral or perhaps even before she passed away. The record is unclear. What is clear is the fact that within days of her death, Henry obviously had changed his mind about his military future and applied for a disability retirement from the Army. A board convened in Philadelphia in May of 1867 with General George G. Meade as chair.[2]

In his petition to the board he described the issues he encountered in warmer climates:

I feel that I have become incapacitated for the performance of the duties required of a Regimental officer, in this climate. In consequence of a wound received in my head at the battle of Corinth, Oct. 4th, 1862. I suffer greatly, at all times, from the effects of excessive heat upon my wound, and when exposed to the heat of the Sun in this climate my suffering is almost unbearable. I can no longer endure any considerable mental or physical exertion without intense suffering. I have at times been affected mentally in a manner which admonishes me that farther continued exertion and exposure to the excessive heat of the Sun in a Southern climate, consequent upon the performance of the duties of an officer in the Army, may produce the most serious results.

It is curious that he did not cite this in his defense during his courts martial. In his opinion, he was suffering from the effects of his wound and did not believe he could function effectively in the warm and humid clime of the Southern United States. To him, it was obvious: let him change station to a more moderate climate or allow him to retire with a disability discharge. It was not so obvious to the Board. There is no evidence as to exactly what Robinett hoped to accomplish or where he hoped to be stationed. What is obvious is that he had had enough of New Orleans and the 1st U.S. Infantry.

The evidence presented at this board sheds a great deal of light on Robinett's conduct and psychological condition from the time of his wounding at Corinth. A medical certificate from Brevet Major Asch Assistant Surgeon, USA, stated the following about his wound:

The track of the wound was in mainly the medial line from left to right. Maj. Robinett has been under my observation since the later part of 1865 and it is my opinion that the effects of said wound renders him unfit for duty in this climate. Extremely hot weather-a mental excitement- renders him nervous and excitable to such a degree as at times to induce fear that the brain may be temporarily affected. Further residence in this climate must do him permanent harm. It is a question whether life in a colder climate will entirely remove the disability.

The wound was far more serious than Robinett first indicated. The surgeon who treated Robinett at Corinth wrote about the nature of the wound:

This is to certify that I attended Lieut (Now Bvt Maj) H.C. Robinett, 1st U.S. Infy. Who was wounded on or about the 4th day of October, 1862 at the battle of Corinth, Miss. He was wounded by a musket ball transing the entire length of the top of his head from before, backwards-completely exposing the bone-No evidence of fracture, could be discerned-He was under my care at Corinth, Miss-until sent North. J.L.G Happensett CPT, Asst. Surgeon.

Captain Williams, Robinett's commander at Corinth, offered supporting testimony:

On the 4th of October 1862 I commanded the 1st U.S. Infantry at the battle of Corinth. The Regt was used as Heavy Artillery. One battery (Battery Robinett) was commanded by 1st Lieut H.C. Robinett 1st U.S. Infantry which battery the enemy charged upon during the battle. 1st Lieut H.C. Robinett was struck by a ball on the top of his head cutting away the scalp and creasing the skull and from which injury he was obliged for a time to retire from the field. Lieut Robinett's conduct during the battle was admirable. He fought his battery very gallantly have had 13 of 26 officers and men who manned the battery either killed or wounded.

On June 8th, Major Robinett appeared before the board to be examined by doctors and questioned about his disability. The surgeons "Find a scar on the median line of the scalp result of a gunshot wound received at Corinth, Miss. Oct. 4th 1862. There is no evidence of any fracture of the skull. From the personal appearance of Major Robinett and from the medical evidence in the case, we are of the opinion that he is not incapacitated from performance of active duty, though service in a hot climate may give use to unpleasant sensations." With that, the board found "that Bvt. Maj. H. C. Robinett, Captain, 1st Infantry, is not incapacitated for active service," and directed Robinett to report to the Adjutant General for orders.

Robinett was devastated. Within a handful of months, he lost his fiancé and his bid to leave honorably the service he loved. He was beside himself with frustration and no small amount of anger. The Army was not seeing things his way. The one hope he still clung to was that the Adjutant General, having read the medical reports, would send him to a milder climate where his wound would not significantly hinder his ability to do his duty.

Judith E. Anderson, in "Haunted Minds: The Impact of Combat Exposure on the Mental and Physical Health of Civil War Veterans" also wrote about PTSD and Civil War veterans in "Years of Suffering and Change: Modern Perspectives on Civil War Medicine," James M. Schmidt and Guy R. Hasegawa (editors), Edinborough Press, 2009. With solid credentials as an experimental psychologist with the Department of Veterans Affairs in New York, her work certainly holds great merit. She has reviewed medical and military records from the war to help draw her observations and conclusions. She clearly indicates that many veterans, and we can assume those like Henry, that remained in the military, suffered invisible wounds from their experiences in combat. Civil War pension boards required objective, physical evidence of wounding. Robinett, based upon his surgeon's testimony, clearly could have proved this. Why this board did not accept the evidence is unfathomable.

Return to Duty

Major Robinett was stunned when he reported for duty and learned he would be returning to the 1st U.S. Infantry and Jackson Barracks in New Orleans. How could this be? How could the Army ignore the evidence presented at the Board hearing by both his surgeons and the examining board and return him to the hot, humid climate of southern Louisiana? There is no evidence to indicate what the Army was thinking, nor why they decided to send him back to New Orleans. Major Robinett packed and returned to New Orleans and arrived on December 31, 1867.

In January of 1868, he wrote another letter to his brother, Theodore. In it he reminisced about happier times,

> *I find my memory carrying me back to the days of our boyhood, when many a pleasant recollection will arise in which you took a very prominent part. Nor do I forget your many Kindnesses to, and acts of self-denial for myself, our dear little sister Lou, and our now aged and beloved parents. I have still the Clothes Brush which you brought from Liverpool. I keep it always with me, and cherish it as a gift from you. It is in an excellent state of preservation, -- in fact it is nearly as good as the day you brought it home to Wilmington. It is a splendid brush – (being useful as well as ornamental) – I think I have never seen a better one. I have with me another article which you used in the days long ago, and which your kindness prompted as a gift to me – your shawl. Do you remember it? – Brown with a brownish-red bar across it. I wore it long and well before coming into the army, since which time I have used it as a blanket. It went every where with me during the war, and is therefore a veteran. I shall keep it as long as I can in remembrance of the giver and the many recollections of pleasure and trials connected with it.*

This is the only letter in which he becomes emotional, but who could blame him after his experiences of the last few years? He was also optimistic about his future, "I hope I may be ordered to the Pacific Coast at some future time...." He concludes the letter with a comment about his fiancé, "I will try and write to you oftener than I have for some time. You know probably what prevented me. It is a sad subject and I do not like to refer to it at all. I am feeling very well now, and I think I am 'all right.'"[3] Robinett was putting on a good face but the turmoil within was evident to those comrades around him.

Endnotes

1. Family Papers, February 13, 1867 letter to Theodore Robinett.

2. Letters Received by the Commission of the Adjutant General's Office, 1861-1870; (National Archives Microfilm Publication Main Series, Roll 578); 1867, 214-279.

3. Family Papers, January 19, 1868 letter to Theodore Robinett.

Chapter IX
"My head, my head, it will burst!"

In the next few months, friends began to notice extremely peculiar behavior patterns. One officer noted, "From the 4th [of January] he was perfectly regular and temperate in his habits. Before that time he was absent for several months. I know that he did not take spirituous liquors during that time. In fact, he hardly ever left the Garrison. I remember many times getting his pay for him and doing various errands for him in the City. He was in his room most of the time when not attending to Company business." He was unable to "foot a short column of figures, and always when he had the slightest mathematical calculation to make, became confused and sent for me to help him out of his difficulty." Robinett also could not "call the multiplications table" to his mind when thus confused. At such times he would clasp his hands over his head and exclaim, "Oh my head, my head, it will burst. It is as hot as fire, I am becoming demented, and yet none of you believe that I am so." One skeptical friend commented about his laments over his wound, "I believe that he allowed himself to so believe, and that he permitted himself to dwell upon the matter and pondered upon it until he actually became insane. He knew that a wound in the head had produced that effect on others, and believed that his confusion and loss of mind were caused from the wound." Another however, took his comments at face value, "In my opinion [the wound] caused his insanity, for there is no doubt of him being insane. No officer in the Regt that knew him had the slightest doubt as to his insanity." One of his closest friends, Captain Leslie Smith, observed his detached demeanor, "I had noticed him for some time previous as being very much changed; at times (he) would act very singular indeed and seemed to be indifferent to what was transpiring around him."[1]

On April 21, 1868, Robinett talked with a Lieutenant Pierce before twilight tattoo.[2] That evening he had received a letter from someone in the family of his fiancé and was also "very much annoyed" about an order to take his company to the field in the coming days as he did not think it was "his detail for detachment duty." According to the Lieutenant, he was talking "in a perfectly normal manner in regard to the different methods of committing suicide." He recalled Henry saying, "Sometimes it takes more courage to live than to die and made use of several similar expressions. He was more calm and self possessed than I had seen him before in a long time." Knowing Robinett's recent behavior and past tribulations, it is hard to believe that Pierce did not recognize him as a man on the brink of ending his life. Robinett left the Lieutenant's room for his and went to bed.

At Jackson Barracks, officer quarters were above the common rooms. Access to these rooms was from an outside set of

Jackson Barracks - Officers Quarters upstairs, common rooms below - Memorial Day 2009

stairs that led to a common porch. The next morning, April 22, 1868, Major Robinett's servant entered his room to black his boots and lay out his clothes. This servant noted that Robinett "looked at him a moment in a wild and terrible manner then turned from him and covered his head with the bed clothes." The servant left his room and within a few seconds, a pistol shot rang out. Lieutenant Pierce wrote to Robinett's father about what transpired next:

Just after Reveille I heard the report of a pistol 2 or 3 shrieks and a noise like the falling of a body on the floor. I immediately went to the room from which the sound proceeded, and saw on the floor Captain Robinett. He was on his back, his legs were straightened, both arms resting on his breast. In his left hand was a Colts Army Revolver, the muzzle of which rested near his right shoulder. There was a bullet wound in the center of his forehead from which blood and brain were oozing. He had evidently stood before his looking glass, held the revolver in his left hand and pulled the trigger with his right hand. There is no doubt about him committing suicide. The surgeon was sent for but it was no use or do anything for him.[3]

Brevet Major Henry C. Robinett expired at 8'oclock "not showing any signs of consciousness or even moving from the time he was discovered until his death." Henry Robinett was just twenty-eight years old.

Captain Smith wrote to his father with the deepest compassion, "The ladies of the post vied with each other in decorating his remains to such an extent that his coffin was literally covered with white roses. Poor fellow, when I took my last look at him as his remains were about being carried off he looked as if he was asleep with a sweet smile playing over his features. I hope his soul is now where we all hope to go in a short time and where trouble and sorrow are not known."[4]

George Avery, who had known Robinett since November of 1863, wrote:

From the histories of like injuries [head wounds] it is a well established truth that the mental equilibrium is very often disturbed, in fact that periodical insanity often follows an injury to the brain. There have been several cases during the last war where the brain had been injured by wounds received in battle causing periodical insanity – and whenever a person is [so] afflicted, it is his due that any unusual deportment should be attributed to the proper exciting cause…Lieutenant Robinett is at times insane, and that at such times he is not responsible for his conduct.

This, written on January 18, 1866, does not appear in any of the court martial documents or in his disability retirement hearing. The only copy exists in his father's pension request file with no indication of to whom it was addressed.

A letter from surgeon S. Catlin, in the same file, discusses his personal observations of Robinett, "from personal observation that he is subject to periodical or temporary insanity…. Cases of periodical insanity arising from injuries of the head and developed by any mental excitement are by no means rare." Another surgeon, C B. White, wrote on the same date, "I have always respected him as a brave soldier and honorable gentleman and here state my firm belief that the indiscretions and improprieties he has recently been guilty of are due to disturbance of the brain and its function, the results of injury received in the U.S. service."

There is no evidence to indicate they were introduced to any governing body or individual during his second court martial. They did find their way into Allen Robinett's pension application in October of 1869, years later. Why these documents were not part of his defense in the third court martial or as part of the petition for remission is open to conjecture; they could have provided significant support in both instances. Where these documents were and why they were not submitted as part of the disability retirement hearing is also a mystery. Were they part of the records of the 1st U.S. at Jackson Barracks and simply kept on file unknown to Robinett?[5] What is obvious is that they would have greatly benefited him in his court martial and with the retirement Board.

Captain Leslie Smith described his relationship with Robinett and showed a completely different perspective:

The major was one of my most intimate acquaintances from the time I first met him in November 1863. In fact, I preferred his society to that of any other of my fellow officers on account of his good moral qualities, such as very few young men of his age and standing in the service possess. It is therefore with painful feelings of sorrow that I inform you that I deeply sympathize with you for the loss of a good kind and affectionate son and with his brother officers for the loss of so honest, upright courteous and gallant gentleman and officer.

Indeed, Robinett possessed all those qualities as more than one person confirmed. His erratic, explosive actions of the past two years do not conform to his generally accepted countenance within his unit.

The most noted surgeon of the period at Jackson Barracks was B.A. Clements. On May 28, 1870, he reflected about Robinett, "His death was caused by a gunshot wound through the skull and brains inflicted by his own hand whilst he was laboring under temporary insanity." On March 2, 1871, he extended his remarks to include, "that he was from time to time under my professional care for some weeks just prior to his death and that he was in an [unstable] state of mind for at least a fortnight before his death." Assuming his account is accurate, why was he ordered to detached duty with his company the day before his death? Was it possible his commanding officer was unaware of his condition? If not, why did Clements not notify his superiors? One would think the unit surgeon would want to notify the command about a soldier so seriously impaired. If they were aware, why did his command not take action and relieve him of his duties? Clements writes again, five months later, about Major Robinett's condition just before his suicide, "His general habits immediately preceding his disease were in every respect excellent." Evidently, before his "temporary insanity" he showed no abnormal behaviors, at least none that Clements could observe. Yet still, in 1866-67, his behavior prompting the courts martial in no way can be considered "excellent." Why did Clements feel the need to amend his comments on two separate occasions?

Clements' post mortem examination indicated that there was "not the slightest depression of the skull and not even the outer plate was fractured." Obviously, his wounding at Corinth did not cause any significant, permanent physical damage, other than his premature frontal balding. Yet there is no doubt something was wrong with Major Robinett. All the signs point towards psychological disorders.

Endnotes

1. Records of the Veterans Administration. Department of the Interior: Pension Office. Record Group 15, Certificate # 153431. Henry's father applied for a pension from the government claiming his son was his sole source of income. Within the file are numerous supporting documents, checks issued on the National Bank of New Orleans from his son that is quite unique. He was granted a pension of $17/month in 1871.

2. Tattoo occurs when a drum or bugle calls soldiers to their barracks for the night.

3. Records of the Veterans Administration. Department of the Interior: Pension Office. Record Group 15, Certificate # 153431.

4. Major Robinett is buried in Chalmette National Cemetery next to the site of the January 8, 1815, Battle of New Orleans. Established in May 1864 as a final resting place for Union soldiers who died in Louisiana during the Civil War, the 15,000 headstones in the cemetery mark the gravesites of veterans of the Spanish-American War, World Wars I and II, and the Vietnam War. Four Americans who fought in the War of 1812 are buried here, though only one of them took part in the Battle of New Orleans. Hurricane Katrina damaged the surrounding walls and a few of the stones but Henry's survived intact. http://www.nps.gov/jela/chalmette-national-cemetery.htm

5. The WPA sponsored a project to record the records of Jackson Barracks. Unfortunately, Hurricane Katrina damaged these volumes to such an extent that they are still under restoration. Only one other known copy exists and resides at LSU.

Chapter X:
After the Battle

The Trauma of Hard War

Numerous studies have explored death in the Civil War, and many have dealt with veterans from the war returning to civilian life. Yet there has been little work on veterans who chose to remain in the Army after the war or specific studies of the Civil War and suicide. Medical records from the period are replete with soldier suicides: Dyer's Compendium[1] is but one example. Drew Gilpin Faust, in her work "This Republic of Suffering,"[2] conducts a fine examination of death in the Civil War, but touches only briefly on suicide. Another interesting study is "Heroes & Cowards: The Social Face of War."[3] This study examines Union soldiers from a statistical perspective to establish a better understanding of societal factors and their impact upon soldiers. Henry fits well into their demographic indicating four out of five white men born between 1837 and 1845 served in the Civil War.[4] Their study of what makes a cohesive company certainly applies to Robinett and the men of C Company, 1st U.S. Infantry, but it is silent on the issue of suicide.

Historian David Silkenat examined suicides in North Carolina after the war. He argues social conditions were a significant factor in post-war suicides. He asserts the war changed the ways in which people understood suicide and that the rate increased, at least in North Carolina, after the war, due to that change. Another factor he attributes this rise to is the gradual shift in the stigma attached to suicide after the war, "It moderates significantly." Even the religious stigma softens after the war. Yet his study, too, does not look at Union soldiers who remained in the service. He does postulate that the returning Confederate soldiers in his study may have exhibited signs of Post Traumatic Stress Disorder (PTSD).

He found three characteristics of returning soldiers, many were wounded, served time in POW camps, and served for an extended period,[5] and Henry Robinett fits two of the three.

Compiling a psychiatric diagnosis after the fact always leaves room for inaccuracy. The only detailed study of PTSD in the Civil War is "Shook Over Hell: Post Traumatic Stress, Vietnam, and the Civil War"[6] by Eric T. Dean Jr. He gleaned core data from the records of Indiana asylums from 1861 to 1919. Dean examines the records of selected mental institutions and their Union Veterans. His work on PTSD and the Civil War Union veteran is detailed and to be commended. He examines the symptoms of PTSD in the context of the retired Civil War veterans. When examined in the context of Robinett's experiences the symptoms seem to strongly indicate PTSD:

-Undergo hardships & trials in the military?	**Yes**
-In a situation where he experienced anxiety & fear?	**Yes**
-Exposed to combat, to death & mutilation of his comrades?	**Yes**
-Exposed to the slaughter of enemy soldiers?	**Yes**
-Encounter disease that might have weakened his psychic defenses?	**Unknown**
-Bonds with friends & family ameliorate his problems or enhance?	**Enhanced - Death of fiancé**
-Did a warm homecoming wash away the pain & deaths?	**Not Documented, unlikely**
-Intrusive recollection-nightmares & flashbacks?	**Not Documented**

-Disoriented thinking?	**Yes**
-Startle reactions?	**Not Documented**
-Social numbing?	**Possible, no indicators**
-Depression (melancholy)?	**Yes**
-Anxiety?	**Yes**
-The "mental distance" from family can be overwhelming?	**Yes**
-Social support?	**Some with fellow officers**
-Fear of:	
Strangers	**Unlikely**
Going outside?	**Jackson Barracks**
Refuse to leave room for days	**Jackson Barracks**
Shun company	**Jackson Barracks**
Fear of recurrence of some great calamity	**Likely**
Think something horrible is going to happen to them	**Likely**
-Descent "into a kind of permanent psychotic state"	**New Orleans**
-Sit for hours alone staring off into space-startled when spoken to.	**Jackson Barracks**
-Dread of calamity, cognitive disorders.	**Yes**
-Parades and welcome home to family does not wash away the "tangle of emotions of devotion, horror, honor, fear, excitement, anger, and boredom."	**Not documented, likely**
-Crying spells, anxiety symptoms	**Yes**
-Nervous behaviors, trembling, shaking, irritability & hyperactivity	**Jackson Barracks**
-Problem with memory or thinking	**Jackson Barracks**

-Inability to concentrate or remember	**Jackson Barracks**
-Loss of memory not associated with any neurological deficit.	**Jackson Barracks**
-Apathetic	**Jackson Barracks**
-Non-military factors –most potent mental shock	**Yes - death of fiancé**
-Gunshot wounds in service	**Corinth**
-Psychological consequences of wound	**New Orleans**
-Restless, sleepless, suicidal	**Jackson Barracks**

Dean also includes significant behavioral descriptors that seem to apply to Robinett:

• Sometimes this fear was so intense that men would fall to the ground paralyzed with terror, bury their face in the grass, grasp the earth, and refuse to move.[7]

• Many experience a sense of disembodiment and become oblivious to their own bodies and needs. Shell or gunshot wounds could bring a man back to the reality of his own body and sense of vulnerability.[8]

• The pounding and concussion from cannonading can be overwhelming.[9]

• Infuriated and obsessed with battle a man can screen out all the horror of death. Concentrate on the matters at hand and put personal safety aside and belatedly react to the horrific scenes they have witnessed.[10]

• Terrifying noise of shells overhead could lead to nervous habits never fully overcome-startle reactions.[11]

• Artillery fire & the sights and sounds of battle could be unnerving in the extreme.[12]

• Perhaps the most horrific aspect of the Civil War experience was the scene of the battlefield after the firing had subsided. Mangled men, dead and dying, littered the landscape.[13]

• One suspects that many cases of men behaving in a disorderly manner or refusing to obey orders ... also involved soldiers who had reached the limits of their endurance, and could easily have been considered psychiatric causalities of war; however these men were punished severely.[14]

• ...many Civil War veterans resorted to suicide as a means of dealing with intolerable mental and physical pain...."[15]

• Pensions were granted for suicide due to war wounds.[16]

Even the terminology of the period describing suspect behavior fits what we know of Robinett based in descriptions by his fellow officers: "The blues, lonesome, disheartened, downhearted, discouraged, demoralized, nervous, played out, used up, anxious, worn down, depressed, rattled, dispirited, sad, melancholy, badly blown, insanity, nostalgia, irritable heart, sunstroke, mania, melancholia, and dementia."[17] Unfortunately, Dean's study does not include soldiers who remained on duty and is quite narrow in its regional scope.

John Keegan wrote concerning the trauma of combat and its effects upon soldiers, "Each moment of combat imposes a strain so great that men will break down in direct relation to the intensity and duration of their exposure...psychiatric causalities are as inevitable as gunshot and shrapnel wounds in warfare."[18] Faust agrees:

Killing was the essence of war. But it also challenged men's most fundamental assumptions about the sanctity of their own and other human lives. Killing produced transformations that were not readily reversible: the living into the dead, most obviously, but the survivors into different men as well, men required to deny, to numb basic human feeling at costs they may have paid for decades after the war ended, as we know twentieth- and twenty-first century soldiers from Vietnam to Iraq continue to do; men who,

like James Garfield, were never quite the same again after seeing
fields of slaughtered bodies destroyed by men just like themselves."[19]

A Union chaplain characterized warfare after Fredericksburg, "A battle is indescribable," we continued, "but once seen it haunts a man till the day of his death."[20]

Confronted with all this overwhelming evidence it appears, from a factual standpoint, Henry Clay Robinett definitely suffered from Post Traumatic Stress Disorder. Seeking confirmation for this lay diagnosis, I contacted four distinguished U.S. Army psychologists. Dr. Bruce A. Leeson, PhD, Clinical Psychologist; Captain Kyle Grohmann, currently immersed in suicide research data for the Army; Dr. John Albrecht, a clinician-researcher "who has been focusing on PTSD as long as many folks have been in practice;" and Ms. Susanne Jones a psychometrician (the measurement of an individual's psychological attributes, including the knowledge, skills, and abilities a professional might need to work in a particular job or profession) all statioined at the Eisenhower Medical Center, Fort Gordon, Georgia.[21]

Though it is difficult to diagnose from the expanse of 141 years, they agreed to meet with me to discuss Robinett. Armed with all my research, documentation, and observations about Henry, I sat down with them for a few hours and supplied them with everything I knew about the Major. I was thoroughly convinced they would confirm my amateur diagnosis. This was not to be the case.

First, PTSD shares some common symptoms with two other conditions: Attention Deficit Disorder and Mild Traumatic Brain Injury (MTBI), what a layperson would call a concussion. After examining the evidence surrounding his wounding at Corinth, these doctors agreed, Henry quite likely experienced MTBI during his brush with death. Certainly, eyewitnesses clearly indicated he was knocked unconscious because of the gunshot to his head and fell under the carriage of one of his guns. This type of concussion is also common in today's Global War on Terror caused by Improvised Explosive Devices (IED). According to Dr. Albrecht:

> *On the head injury question, there is some question today about the extent of damage in Mild Traumatic Brain Injury; now attributing the presumed behavioral effects as more likely due to psychological causes rather than to brain damage. One recent study indicated that about 89% of combat-related head injuries were in the mild range (in the current War on Terror). The extent of the injury can to some extent be inferred from the immediate effects--loss of consciousness, dizziness, nausea, slowed thinking and difficulty concentrating, loss of memory for a circumscribed period of time preceding, during, and after the head injury.*[22]

They were inclined to rule out PTSD as a likely diagnosis since there was nothing to suggest any reliving of his wounding or excessive preoccupation with his experiences during the war, common characteristics of PTSD. Nor is hypervigilance or risk aversion evident in his experiences. In addition, neither is inappropriate appraisal of risk when risk would otherwise be minimal is evident in any in Robinett's behavior. There is nothing even remotely to suggest an excessive preoccupation with his experiences, another significant symptom of PTSD. Indeed, he never wrote of his wartime experiences except a few small encounters; one while delivering a message for General Grant and a rather uneventful experience in Louisiana travelling through "The Pass." His response to inquiries was typical among Civil War soldiers, feeling no need to detail his experiences since his family "have, no doubt, read it in all the newspapers."

According to the Centers For Disease Control, "MTBI symptoms may appear mild, but they can lead to significant, life-long impairment in an individual's ability to function physically, cognitively, and psychologically....Data suggests that as many as 75% of all brain injured people sustain MTBI....An unknown proportion of those who are not hospitalized may experience long-term problems such as: confusion, cognitive and/or memory problems, fatigue, changes in sleep patterns, mood changes...."[23] Certainly MTBI is a much more likely diagnoses in Robinett's case. Numerous witnesses recount that he was unconscious lying under the gun carriage and most surely had a concussion caused by the impact of the ball.

While the inability to manage anger is a marker of PTSD, it also can be symptomatic of numerous other conditions. Of all the potential symptoms of PTSD, the only one that he possessed was his problem managing anger, which is not specific to PTSD- it could indicate problems with narcissistic personality traits, or impulsivity, secondary to traumatic brain injury, or simply what is termed intermittent explosive disorder. Towards the end of our discussions, Captain Grohmann leaned forward and said, "He is a narcissist, his letters and behavior point towards it." Narcissism is a personality disorder where someone has an excessive fascination with one's self or in other words, self-love. Robinett most definitely fits into this category.

This revelation shed light on much of Henry's words and actions. In his first letter from DMA to his father concerning his grades he wrote, "I believe I have been perfect." Indeed, simply the act of going to Secretary of War Simon Cameron's office and asking for an appointment points towards narcissism, he was going to the top to get what he wanted, a regular Army commission. His reference in his letters to his "enemies" and his triumph over them and the fact that he could not see the impact he was having on others around him also point towards narcissism. As Dr. Albrecht said of the Varieties Theatre affair, "He was a Boston Red Sox fan in Yankee Stadium." Robinett could not understand how the simple act of applauding and yelling "encore" could incite the unreconstructed Southerners in the attendance. He could not see why DeRussy was such a thorn in his side nor how the courts martial could possibly find against him. For him, the only logical conclusion was they were his enemies. He used his influence in Wilmington politics and with General Grant to have the cases mitigated. Robinett yelled, as he was being mishandled in the Varieties incident that he was a friend of General Grant and he was going to let him know about such shameful treatment of a friend of his. There is not one shred of evidence that he was a true "friend" of Grant, indeed it is quite unlikely that Grant would even remember much about his one-time "extra" aide-de-camp. He was only with Grant for a short period during the final few months of the war and Grant never mentions him in his correspondence. Blinded by narcissism, Robinett could not recognize the effects his actions and comments had upon others.

The fact that Robinett committed suicide while observing the act in his mirror is a unique aspect of his suicide. There is very little work on suicide while looking in a mirror as of this writing. In Alabama from 1983 to 1987, there were 334 cases of suicide and of those only eleven cases where a mirror was involved. From a psychological point of view, the mirror represents the "soul's image." When looking in a mirror, people do not see themselves as they truly are. They see the way they think they appear. Perhaps he had to visualize himself physically in the mirror in order to be able to kill himself. Projecting from first person to second may be the psychic mechanism that enabled him to take his life.[24] Another possibility is that Henry was so dejected at the numerous ego-shattering events of the past three years that weighed so heavily upon him that he decided to look in the mirror to be sure he, at least, got this one act correct. Viewing his own suicide is bizarre in the extreme and may indicate he was psychotic and likely out of touch with reality. Since he was probably narcissistic, he may have wanted to kill himself correctly without "messing it up" and used the mirror as a guide, indicating he was a perfectionist as is often seen in the narcissistic personality disorder. There is no evidence to conclude Robinett was a masochist. It is likely Robinett was so disappointed with himself, his honor so impugned, that he punished himself by not only taking his life but also watching himself die. Finally, did he look in the mirror in order to aim at the spot where the headaches originated? Was shooting himself in the head a way of ridding himself of the headaches? Perhaps Robinett was trying to free himself from the pain by shooting it.

Unfortunately, long distance psychiatry has no definitive answers for us.[25]

It is also glaringly obvious that Robinett had serious anger management issues after the war. This can be attributed to narcissistic rage. Rage, deep seated in the core of one's personality, is exasperated in a narcissist who feels unjustifiably wronged. You can clearly read in his defense writings his indignation at all the accusations. The fact that Robinett was obviously unable to control his rage in all three incidents clearly indicates he was incapable, at times, of thinking rationally and his rage, most likely, an outgrowth of narcissism fed by wartime success and a modicum of fame and acclaim. His personality, shaped by family, war, and training impacted his post war actions.

After the Battle

Post-war events combined with his inner-self, conspired to bring Major Robinett down. Robinett, quite possibly, would have gotten himself into trouble wherever he was. The hatred that was New Orleans and the animosity of some officers in the Gulf District were not an affirmative atmosphere for Henry. In his eyes, he was demoted two grades to First Lieutenant for, "If I had had political influence I could at least have been a Brig-Gen two years ago." He initiates a confrontation with a Major, refusing to obey his orders, "You are not my commanding officer. I will not respect your authority." Then, only a few weeks later, turns an offer of camaraderie with two veterans into a verbal confrontation with not only the bartender but, again, with a superior officer, Captain DeRussy, "calculated to prejudice his authority over said enlisted men and incite a mutinous spirit on their part." After employing the influence of his friends and his reinstatement, as a "Red Sox fan in Yankee Stadium" he could not understand why he was so wronged by the citizenry of New Orleans and DeRussy a second time, "God damn him, he [DeRussy] is no soldier! He is a sycophant." Furthermore, taking the three affairs collectively, "I was persecuted by a set of military tyrants and mean, unprincipled, and envious beings, miscalled men and gentlemen." These accusations were simply incorrect and a distortion of the facts. Robinett could not envision the possibly that he could have done anything wrong or offensive in any of the three incidents. "It's not my fault" was no doubt his mantra.

Where exactly his breaking point occurred is open to conjecture. Was it the indignity of the "demotion," the affront to his honor by those that questioned him, or was it when the people of New Orleans decided to "throw the bum out!" It might have been with the death of his fiancé or his reassignment back to New Orleans after his disability discharge hearing. From a distance, we cannot possibly determine what specifically was the trigger of his demise. With improved, sophisticated psychiatric services, it might have been possible to diagnose his illness and to treat his issues effectively, but not in the mid-nineteenth century.

His training at Delaware Military Academy and his early military career provided him the tools necessary to fight his unit successfully at every turn. His performance during the war, in the line of duty and under fire, cannot possibly be questioned. In combat, he behaved honorably and with great courage. He exhibited all the qualities of an effective, capable officer. He was praised by his superiors on numerous occasions and received two brevets, so it seems that he more than adequately performed his duties. His conduct at Corinth in Battery Robinett and at Vicksburg during the assault on the 2nd Texas lunette are in the finest traditions of the United States Army. As aide-de-camp to General Grant, Robinett proved himself capable, responsible, and efficient in carrying out his duties. When he needed General Grant or his Chief of Staff, General John Rawlings, to assist in clearing his name, they were more than willing to use their influence to mitigate his punishments and return him to service; General Meade proved to be less kind. Fellow Freemason, Andrew Johnson, like Grant and Stanton, also was amenable to granting Robinett mitigation. The ties that Robinett carefully built during the war served him well afterwards.

The final court martial is even more difficult to fathom. While Robinett should never have placed himself in such a position, the court surely was aware of the hostile climate in the city of New Orleans. The mood of the citizenry was not a subtle undercurrent but rather a boiling cauldron of hate towards the United States government in general and the Army in specific. The testimony of both the police officer and usher, especially after their admission of service in the Confederate Army, should have been suspect. Why the court placed more credence in the words of Rebel civilians over their own officers present at the encounter is incomprehensible. These officers corroborated Henry's account, yet were ignored. General Sheridan's refusal to review or mitigate the case also indicates a breakdown in command authority and responsibility. Sheridan's harsh judgment appears overtly punitive under questionable circumstances. Perhaps he was tired of dealing with this young officer and saw this as a way to remove Robinett from his command.

Taking these incidents and the death of his fiance into account, it is no wonder Robinett applied for a disability retirement and an honorable way out of the Army. Why he did not submit the written statements from three of his 1st U.S. surgeons detailing his mental capacity can be attributed to his unwillingness to admit such a weakness as a point of honor. What cannot be understood is why the Army and General Meade clearly rejected the findings of both the board's own surgeons and the witnesses Robinett presented. All the evidence presented clearly indicated that his wounding at Corinth made it extremely difficult for him to function effectively in a climate such as New Orleans offers. Without a doubt, at the least, his request for service in a mild climate held merit. His service during the war was commendable and without question, it was only after the war that Robinett's actions become erratic and irrational. Failing to grant his retirement, it was incumbent upon the Army to ensure Robinett's effectiveness as an officer by reassigning him to a more moderate climate where his head wound would not be such a mitigating factor. It is impossible to assign any logical rationale for the Adjutant General assignment of Robinett back to New Orleans and the 1st U.S. Infantry after all the evidence presented at the hearing. What does the military owe its soldiers who decide to remain in service to their country after a war? It would seem much more than they provided Robinett. His service noted and taken into account would have gone a long way to preventing his suicide and retaining his services as a capable, effective officer.

Henry Robinett's sense of honor played a decisive role during his troubles after the war and throughout his entire life. Trained at Delaware Military Academy in the ways of an honorable officer and gentleman, inured by the United States Army early in his career, enhanced by his actions at Corinth and Vicksburg, he became a capable, competent officer, cited for his bravery; everything he wished to become. Anchored by the teachings of Colonel Hyatt, Freemasonry, and the Holy Trinity Church, Robinett, felt deeply wronged when his sense of honor and decency were utterly trampled by "his enemies." In the end, his attempt to leave the Army with a modicum of dignity through the disability retirement board was rejected out of hand. The surgeons of the 1st U.S. were aware of his mental instability, yet chose to remain silent, at least in official channels. Coupled with a return to the hotbed of New Orleans, the loss of his fiancé, and new orders to take to the field in Louisiana, Robinett felt compelled to end a life in "the last sad hour of freedom's dream."

Finally, what role and responsibility did the United States Army and its leadership have in Henry Robinett's demise? The Army failed this veteran combat officer. Should a slot have been found at the rank of Captain in another unit? Numerous officers received a reduction of more than one grade after the war; Robinett did not adjust as well as most. It might have been possible but should not have been necessary. Clearly Robinett knew this might happen and should have accepted his reduction in rank, but his narcissism would not allow him to do so. There can be no doubt that Robinett deserved his first rebuke for the confrontation with Major Maloney but the harsh treatment at the hands of the second court marital can be easily questioned. Does a decorated officer of some renown deserve dismissal for questionable actions? Two men, in a heated confrontation, are unlikely to remember exactly what words they uttered. Since the incident turned on those exact words and neither had corroborating witnesses, it is hard to fathom why the judgment was so extreme. In addition, it would seem the Army could have reassigned Robinett to a different unit after this confrontation in order to prevent future animosity. The Army, no doubt, followed "the book" in the case of Robinett but there are times the book is too inflexible and unable to adapt to current conditions and circumstances.

What did the United States government owe Robinett and other veterans in the area of mental health care? With the state of psychiatry in the mid-nineteenth century the answer is probably little, as little was known about the issues intense combat could cause. At the time, no one was aware of PTSD, MTBI, or the myriad of other psychological conditions produced by the horrors of combat. If the Army surgeons in New Orleans had been more pro-active in their treatment of Robinett and discussed his condition with his superior officers, they could have prevented his collapse or, at the least, had him relieved from duty. The Army must assume some responsibility for his eventual suicide. Perhaps, if the U.S. Army had a program to assist veterans with issues resulting from the carnage of war and if his friends and associates had recognized his mental state for what it really was, his life could have been saved. He would then have been afforded the opportunity for a successful post-war career and lived the long life he dreamed of so often. How many other soldiers fell into this trap?

Henry Robinett's story also highlights many of the issues for occupation soldiers in a hostile city. Today the echoes of such events can be heard in Baghdad, Ramadi, Tikrit, and Kandahar. New Orleans was a city hostile to the soldiers of the United States Army in every way. A city full of racial animosity and conflicted values. These soldiers were expected to maintain order and extend the authority of the U.S. government without any experience or training in the effective methods necessary to perform their duties.

Today's Army, deeply immersed in a near epidemic of suicide among its soldiers, is working diligently to address the issue. In a recent pamphlet issued by the Department of the Army it states, "The key to the prevention of suicide is positive leadership and deep concern by supervisors of military personnel and DA civilian employees who are at increased risk of suicide."[26] This was lacking in the 1860s. It continues:

Factors contributing to suicide are said to include loneliness ("an emotional state in which a person experiences powerful feelings of emptiness and spiritual isolation"), worthlessness ("an emotional state in which an individual lacks any feelings of being valued by others"), hopelessness ("a strong sense of futility, due to the belief that the future holds no escape from current negative circumstances"), helplessness, and guilt ("a strong sense of shame associated with actions they believe are wrong").[27]

All of these factors existed in Henry Robinett and, in all cases, were observed by his associates or doctors. Finally, on the detection and prediction of suicide the pamphlet states:

Some suicides may be expected even in units with the best leadership climate and most efficient crisis intervention and suicide prevention programs. Therefore, it is important to redefine the goal of suicide prevention as being suicide risk reduction [which] consists of reasonable steps taken to lower the probability that an individual will engage in acts of self-destructive behavior.[28]

The doctors assigned to the 1st U.S. Infantry were unable to reduce the risk of suicide in Robinett's case when even a few "reasonable steps" might have prevented his untimely demise. Nineteenth century psychiatry was just not yet prepared to deal with the lasting effects of the trauma of war.

"Oh! Who would live a slave in this?"

Henry Clay Robinett's life was marked by periods of uncertainty, strife, and sheer terror. His education at Delaware Military Academy more than adequately prepared him for military life and the trials of nineteenth century warfare. Though he began drilling with a broomstick in Delaware, his experiences led him to a redoubt at Corinth and his "pet Parrots." Here a Minnie ball to the head in the middle of the carnage that was Battery Robinett sealed his fate and set his life's course. He was forever altered as he struggled to understand these changes within him for the rest of his short life.

During his time at DMA, Robinett, no doubt, studied the great writers from Europe; Sir Thomas Moore was one of those writers. In *After the Battle,* Moore describes the scene as night closes around the conquering hero. Henry, obviously moved by this poem, chose to use a short passage in his defense at his final court martial. There is no evidence that Robinett was contemplating suicide at that point, yet the words of Moore read like his eulogy. Only after death was his tortured soul free.

After the Battle
Sir Thomas Moore

Night closed around the conqueror's way,
And lightnings showed the distant hill,
Where those who lost that dreadful day,
Stood few and faint, but fearless still.
The soldier's hope, the patriot's zeal,
For ever dimmed, for ever crost--
Oh! who shall say what heroes feel,
When all but life and honor's lost?

The last sad hour of freedom's dream,
And valor's task, moved slowly by,
While mute they watcht, till morning's beam
Should rise and give them light to die.
There's yet a world, where souls are free,
Where tyrants taint not nature's bliss;--
If death that world's bright opening be,
Oh! who would live a slave in this?

Chalmette National Military Cemetery, Memorial Day 2009

145

Henry Clay Robinett as a Lieutenant- courtesy of Pacific University

In 1963, PMC cadets organized Battery Robinett. To this day, the cannon is still fired at football games. Courtesy of Widener University Archive

Battery Robinett, Homecoming 2009

Endnotes

1. Dyer, Fredrick H. "Compendium of the War of The Rebellion." Cedar Rapids, Iowa: Torch Press, 1908.

2. Faust, Drew Gilpin. "This Republic of Suffering: Death and the American Civil War." New York: Alfred A. Knopf, 2008.

3. Costa, Dora L. and Matthew E. Khan. "Cowards and Heroes: Group loyalty in the American Civil War." Princeton, New Jersey: Princeton University Press, 2008.

4. Ibid, p. 56.

5. David Silkenat, North Carolina Public Radio-WUNC Frank Stasio, May 21 2008 broadcast.

6. Dean, Eric T. Jr. "Shook Over Hell Post-Traumatic Stress: Vietnam, and the Civil War." Cambridge, Massachusetts: Harvard University Press, 1997.

7. Ibid. 54.

8. Ibid, 55-56.

9. Ibid. 57.

10. Ibid.

11. Ibid. 63.

12. Ibid. 66.

13. Ibid.

14. Ibid. 125.

15. Ibid, 156.

16. Ibid., 158

17. Ibid. 115.

18. Keegan, John, "The Face of Battle." (New York: Random House, 1976), p. 329.

19. Faust, 60.

20. Ibid. 209.

21. Dr. Leeson indicated before our discussions: "We do need to be absolutely clear that we come as individuals and speak each for ourselves. We do not represent the U.S. Army, Eisenhower Army Medical Center or Fort Gordon. We are coming to address issues raised by an historic individual in light of current research and scientific understanding. Nothing we say can be used to draw inferences, conclusions or make statements about the current situation in the U.S. Armed Forces, nor can any statement be allowed about Soldiers in the current conflicts." I would like to thank each of these fine doctors for all of their assistance in shedding light on Robinett's condition.

22. E-mail conservation from Dr Albrecht Tue 9/1/2009.

23. Centers for Disease Control and Prevention, Heads Up: facts for Physicians About Mild Traumatic Brain Injury. http://www.cdc.gov/TraumaticBrainInjury/pdf/Facts_for_Physicians_booklet-a.pdf   accessed 1 September 2009.

24. Riddick, LeRoy, Pamela G. Mussell, Gary D. Cumberland. "The Mirror's Use in Suicide." The American Journal of Forensic Medicine and pathology. Volume 10, Issue 1, 1989. Section 2-2, a, p. 8.

25. I also discussed Robinett's condition with was Colonel Philip A. Horton, Medical Director of the Residential Treatment Facility, Eisenhower Medical Hospital, Ft. Gordon, GA. He also has extensive work with suicidal patients.

26. Department of the Army. Pamphlet 600–24 Health Promotion, Risk Reduction, and Suicide Prevention. Section 2-2.a, 24 November, 2009.

27. Ibid. 3-2, p. 10-11.

28. Ibid. 2-2, a, P. 8.

Bibliography

Primary Sources

Blue and Gray Educational Society. *The Corinth Diary of Private Charles Stevens.* Saline, Michigan: McNaughton & Gunn, 2006.

Byers, Samuel H.M. Major. *With Fire and Sword.* New York: Neale Publishing Company, 1911.

Christian, William Capt. *Captain William Christian of Company A on the Battle of Shiloh.* Tri-Weekly Telegraph. Houston, Texas, July 4, 1862.

Dyer, Fredrick H. *Compendium of the War of The Rebellion.* Cedar Rapids, Iowa: Torch Press, 1908.

Heitman, Francis B. *Historical Register and Dictionary of the United States Army From its Organization, September 29, 1789, to March 2, 1903.* Vol. 1 Washington: Government Printing Office, 1903.

Jackson, David, Prentice, ed. *The colonel's diary; journals kept before and during the civil war by the late Colonel Oscar L. Jackson...sometime commander of the 63rd regiment O. V. I.* Sharon, PA: 1922.

Labuzan, Charles C. 1st Lt. *Letter.* Greenville Dodge Papers, Iowa State Historical Library.

Letters Received by the Commission of the Adjutant General's Office, 1861-1870; (National Archives Microfilm Publication Main Series, Roll 578); 1867, 214-279.

Letters Received by the Commission of the Adjutant General's Office, 1863-1870; (National Archives Microfilm Publication M1064, Roll 106); 1864, M136 – M576.

Letters Received by the Commission of the Adjutant General's Office, 1863-1870; (National Archives Microfilm Publication M1064, Roll 116); 1864, R208—R502.

Letters Received by the Commission of the Adjutant General's Office, 1863-1870; (National Archives Microfilm Publication M1064. Roll 150); 1865, C166 – C365.

Letters Received by the Commission of the Adjutant General's Office, 1863-1870; (National Archives Microfilm Publication M1064, Roll 163); 1865, G1 – G224.

Letters Received by the Commission of the Adjutant General's Office, 1863-1870; (National Archives Microfilm Publication M1064, Roll 207); 1865, R180 – R311.

Letters Received by the Commission of the Adjutant General's Office, 1863-1870; (National Archives Microfilm Publication M1064, Roll 121); 1865, R755 – R919.

Letters Received by the Commission of the Adjutant General's Office, 1863-1870; (National Archives Microfilm Publication M1064, Roll 125); 1865, S389—S597.

Letters Received by the Commission of the Adjutant General's Office, 1863-1870; (National Archives Microfilm Publication M1064, Roll 129); 1866, R5—R364.

Lyarger, E. L. *The Battle of Corinth*. National Tribune, November 26, 1908.

McKinstry, J.A. *With Col. Rogers When He Fell.* Confederate Veteran, Vol. 4, No. 7, Nashville, July 1896.

Minturn, W.H.H. "Battle of Corinth, Fuller's Ohio Brigade and the Part it Took in This Engagement." *National Tribune*, May 23, 1901.

Moore, J. C. Gen. *Some Confederate War Incidents,* Confederate Veteran, Volume XII, March, 1904.

Records of the Office of the Judge Advocate General Court Martial Case Files, 1809-1894; (National Archives Record Group 153, File OO-1898.

Records of the Office of the Judge Advocate General Court Martial Case Files, 1809-1894; (National Archives Record Group 153, File MM-3435.

Records of the Veterans Administration. Department of the Interior: Pension Office. Record Group 15, Certificate # 153431.

Regimental Files, 1st U.S. Siege Guns, Folder 532, Vicksburg National Military Park.

Register of Bayard Family Papers, *Letter John Dale to Thomas F. Bayard 29 JAN 1861.* The Delaware Historical Society. Wilmington, DE.

Register of the Graduates and Ex-Cadets of the Pennsylvania Military College That Have Served or Are Now in Service in the Army and Navy of the United States or in the National Guard. Widener University Archives.

Register of the Robinette Family Papers, 1845-1910 University of the Pacific Holt-Atherton Department of Special Collections University Library Mss183 [Identification of item], Robinette

Family Papers, Mss183, Holt-Atherton Department of Special Collections, University of the Pacific Library.

Rogers, William P. Col. *Letter from Rogers to his Wife, May 1, 1862.* William P. Rogers Papers, Eugene C. Barker, Texas History Center, University of Texas, Austin, Texas.

Stevens, Charles. *The Corinth Diary of Private Charles Stevens Company A, 47th Illinois Infantry.* Danville, VA: Blue and Gray Education Society, 2006.

U.S. War Department. A Compilation of the *Official Record of the Union and Confederate Armies.* Washington: GPO, 1880-1901.

War Department, Surgeon General's Office. *A Report on Barracks and Hospitals with Descriptions of Military Posts.* Washington, D.C.: Government Printing Office, 1870.

Widener University Archives. *Pennsylvania Military Academy Course Catalogs, 1859 – 1881 Rules and Regulations.* Chester, PA.

Secondary Sources

Allen, Stacy D. "Crossroads of the Western Confederacy" Blue & Gray Magazine Visitor's Guide-Corinth Mississippi. 2007.

Anderson, Judith E., *Haunted Minds: The Impact of Combat Exposure on the Mental and Physical Health of Civil War Veterans* found in *Years of Suffering and Change: Modern Perspectives on Civil War Medicine*, James M. Schmidt and Guy R. Hasegawa (editors), Edinborough Press, 2009.

Andrew, Rod Jr. *Long Gray Lines: Southern Military School Tradition, 1839-1915.* Chapel Hill, NC: The University of North Carolina Press, 2001.

Arnold, James R. *Grants Wins the War: Decision at Vicksburg.* New York: John Wiley & Sons, Inc., 1997.

Askew, Samuel L. *An Analysis of Unit Cohesion in the 42nd Alabama Infantry.* Master's Thesis for U.S. Army Command and General Staff College. Fort Leavenworth, Kansas: unpublished, 2003.

Ballard, Michael B. *Vicksburg: The Campaign That Opened the Mississippi.* Chapel Hill, NC: University of North Carolina Press, 2004.

Buxton, Henry J. *Pennsylvania Military College, The Story of One Hundred Years 1821-1921.* Chester, PA: 1921.

Carter, Samuel III. *The Final Fortress: Vicksburg.* New York: St. Martin's Press, 1980.

Catton, Bruce. *America Goes to War: The Civil War and Its Meaning in American Culture.* Hanover, NH: Wesleyan University Press, 1986.

Chance, Joseph E. *The Second Texas Infantry: From Shiloh to Vicksburg.* Austin, TX: Eakin Press, 1984.

Clinton, Catherine. *Southern Families at War: Loyalty and Conflict in the Civil War South.* Oxford: Oxford University Press, 2000.

Cockrell, Monroe F. *The Lost Account of the Battle of Corinth and the Court Martial of Gen. Van Dorn.* Jackson, TN: Mercer Press, 1855.

Commager, Henry Steele. "Rosecrans Whips Van Dorn at Corinth," from *The Blue and The Gray.* Indianapolis, Indiana: Bobbs-Merrill Co., 1950.

Conrad, James Lee. *The Young Lions: Confederate Cadets at War.* Mechanicsburg, PA: Stackpole, 1997.

Cooling, B. Franklin, III. *Delaware Military Academy, 1859-1862.* *Delaware History 14, no. 3 (1971).*

Cornelison, John E. Jr., Tammy D. Cooper. *Archeological Investigations of Battery Robinett and the Confederate Attack on Corinth.* Shiloh National Military Park, 2004.

Costa, Dora L. and Matthew E. Khan. *Cowards and Heroes: Group loyalty in the American Civil War.* Princeton, New Jersey: Princeton University Press, 2008.

Cotton, Robert I. Jr., Mary Ellen Hayward. *Maryland in the Civil War: A House Divided*, Baltimore, MD: Maryland Historical Society, 1994.

Cozzens, Peter. *The Darkest Days of the War: The Battles of Iuka & Corinth.* Chapel Hill: University of North Carolina Press, 1997.

Dean, Eric T. Jr. *Shook Over Hell Post-Traumatic Stress: Vietnam, and the Civil War.* Cambridge, Massachusetts: Harvard University Press, 1997.

Department of the Army. Pamphlet 600–24 *Health Promotion, Risk Reduction, and Suicide Prevention.* November, 2009.

Donovan, James A. *Militarism*, U.S.A. New York: Charles Scribner's Sons, 1970.

Dossman, Steven Nathaniel. *Campaign for Corinth: Blood in Mississippi.* Abilene, TX: McWhiney Foundation Press, 2006

Easterlin, Richard A. "Regional Income Trends, 1840-1950." In *The Reinterpretation of American Economic History*, edited by Robert W. Fogel and Stanley L. Engerman. New York: Harper and Row, 1972.

Faust, Drew Gilpin. *This Republic of Suffering: Death and the American Civil War*. New York: Alfred A. Knopf, 2008.

Franklin, John Hope. *The Militant South, 1800-1860*. Boston, MA: Beacon Press, 1956.

Grabau, Warren E. *Ninety-Eight days: A Geographer's View of the Vicksburg Campaign*. Knoxville, TN: The University of Tennessee Press, 2000.

Green, Jennifer R. *Military Education and the Emerging Middle Class in the Old South*. Cambridge, England: Cambridge University Press, 2008.

Handbook of Texas Online. Rogers, William Peleg. http://www. tshaonline.org/handbook/online/articles/RR/fro64.html. accessed 7 July 2009.

Hess, Earl J. *Field Armies and Fortifications in the Civil War*. Chapel Hill, North Carolina: University of North Carolina Press, 2005.

Higginbotham, R. Don. "The Martial Spirit in the Antebellum South: Some Further Speculations in a National Context." *Journal Southern History* 58, no 1. (February 1992).

Hogue, James K. *Uncivil War: Five New Orleans Street Battles and the Rise and Fall of Radical Reconstruction*. Baton Rouge: Louisiana State University Press, 2006.

Hollandsworth, James G. Jr. *An Absolute Massacre: The New Orleans Race Riot of July 30, 1866*. Baton Rouge, LA: Louisiana State University, 2001.

House, James K. *Uncivil War: Five New Orleans Street Battles and the Rise and Fall of Radical Reconstruction.* Baton Rouge: Louisiana State University Press, 2006.

Johnson, Robert Underwood. *Battles and Leaders of the Civil War VOL II.* New York : The Century Co., 1887-1888.
Karsten, Peter. *The Military in America.* 2nd Ed. New York: Free Press, 1986.

Kett, Joseph F. *Rites of Passages: Adolescence in America, 1790 to the Present.* New York: Basic Books, 1977.

Kimmel, Michael. *Manhood in America: A Cultural History.* New York: Free Press, 1996.

McPherson, James M. *What They Fought For 1861-1865.* New York: Anchor Books, 1995.

Mann, Horace. *The Republic and the School: Horace Mann on the Education of Free Men.* Edited by Lawrence A Cremin. New York: Teachers College Press, 1957.

Moll, Clarence Russell. *A History of Pennsylvania Military College.* Ph.D. diss. New York University, 1954.

Nosworthy, Brent. *The Bloody Crucible of Courage: Fighting Methods and Combat Experience of the Civil War.* New York: Carroll & Graf, 2003.

O'Leary, Cecilia Elizabeth. *To Die For: The Paradox of America Patriotism.* Princeton, N.J.: Princeton University Press, 1999.

Pearson, Alden B., Jr. "Middle-class, Border-state Family during the Civil War" In *The Southern Common People: Studies in Nineteenth-century Social History*, edited by Edward Magdol and Jon L. Wakelyn. Westport, CT: Greenwood Press, 1980.

Pugh, David. *Sons of Liberty: The Masculine Mind in Nineteenth-century America.* Westport, CT: Greenwood Press, 1983.

Reed, Thomas J., W. Andrew McKay, Rev. Anthony R. Wade. *Untying the Political Knot: Delaware During the War Between the States.* Wilmington, NC: Broadfoot Publishing Co., 2001.

Robertson, James I., Jr. *Soldiers Blue and Gray.* Columbia, SC: University of South Carolina Press, 1998.

Rodenbough, Theophilus Francis, William L Haskin eds. *The Army of the United States, Historical Sketches of Staff and Line with Portraits of Generals-in-Chief.* New York: Maynard, Merrill, & Co. 1896.

Rotundo, E. Anthony. *American Manhood: Transformation in Masculinity from the Revolution to the Modern Era.* New York: Basic Books, 1993.

Scharff, J. Thomas. *History of Delaware 1609-1888.* Philadelphia: L.J. Richards & Co. 1888.

Shambaugh, Benjamin F. *Biographies and Portraits of the Progressive Men of Iowa.* Vol. 11 Des Moines: Conaway & Shaw, 1899.

Silkenat, David. North Carolina Public Radio-WUNC. Frank Stasio and Lindsay Thomas. May 21, 2008 broadcast.

Storey, Margaret M. "Civil War Unionists and the Political Culture of Loyalty in Alabama 1960-61." *Journal of Southern History.* vol. LXIX, no. 1. (February 2003).

Tunnell, Ted. *Crucible of Reconstruction: War, Radicalism, and Race in Louisiana 1862-1877.* Baton Rouge, LA: Louisiana State University, 1984.

Wakelyn, Jon L. "Antebellum College Life and the Relations between Fathers and Sons." In *The Web of Southern Social Relations: Women, Family, and Education*, edited by J. Fraser Jr., R. Frank Saunders Jr., and Jon Wakelyn, Athens: University of Georgia Press, 1985.

Warmoth, Henry Clay. *War, Politics, and Reconstruction: Stormy Days in Louisiana*. Columbia, SC: University of South Carolina Press, 2006.

Wiley, Bell Irvin. *The Life of Billy Yank: The Common Soldier of the Union*. Baton Rouge, LA: Louisiana State University Press, 1971.

Wiley, Bell Irvin. *The Life of Johnny Reb: The Common Soldier of the Confederacy*. Baton Rouge, LA: Louisiana State University Press, 1978.

Williams, Joy "One Acre," *Harper's*, February 2001.

About the Author

Bill Speer graduated from Pennsylvania Military College in 1972. Since then, he has worn many hats.

He has a master's in Military Studies from American Military University and currently serves as the Global War on Terror military historian for JANUS Research Group, Inc. and supports the United States Army Signal Corps historian. He is also an instructor at the American Military University and previously taught at the community college level and various public schools. He served as historian for the Defenders of American Naval Museum and as the Online Educational Coordinator for the United States Civil War Center at LSU. Speer was a member of the Advisory Board for the Texas State Historical Society and on the Educational Advisory Board for the Fort Bend County, TX Museum. He also served as a textbook reviewer for Prentice Hall.

Mr. Speer has worked with the National History Day foundation for two decades, teaching history to our future leaders. Bill has an intensive background in Holocaust studies and was a participant in the Holocaust Survivors Study Program in Poland and Israel. He also has over thirty five years of military simulation development and implementation. In conjunction with the Defenders of American Naval Museum, he worked on the restoration of PT 309 which now resides at the Pacific War Museum in Fredericksburg, Texas and PT-305 which is now under final restoration at the National D-Day Museum in New Orleans. He also developed websites and programs for the Institute of Texan Cultures in San Antonio, TX.

Upon retirement from public education, Bill was a professional tournament bass fisherman and a full-time fishing guide before joining JANUS. He currently resides in Harlem, Georgia near Fort Gordon and the United States Army Signal Center. He is an avid wargamer and has assisted in the development of numerous simulations relating to World War II and the American Civil War.